RESIL
PENWITH
2012

CW01514197

Edited by the Transition Penwith Team

TRANSITION *Penwith*

Resilient Penwith 2012

Edited by The Transition Penwith Team

First published

2012

Transition Penwith
care of Penwith Centre
Parade Street
Penzance
Cornwall
TR18 4BU
www.transitionpenwith.org.uk
info@transitionpenwith.org.uk

ISBN

978-0-9570787-0-3

Typesetting, Design and Layout

Jonathan How
www.coherentvisions.com

Bookshop Distribution

Edge of Time Ltd
BCM Edge
London
WC1N 3XX
www.edgeoftime.co.uk

Contents

Contents

Fair for the Future 2010, held near St Just

Introduction

Welcome to this first book from Transition Penwith. If you have not heard of the Transition Movement before then you are probably wondering what on earth it's all about... what is it a transition from and – more importantly – what is it a transition to? And why should you be interested anyway?

Well, the Transition Movement is not all hippies and tree huggers! At its core, Transition could be described as 'progressive pragmatism' or 'radical realism': it is firmly rooted in a hard-headed assessment of present and future constraints in our energy, climate and economy and is concerned with developing and promoting effective and resilient responses to those interconnected challenges.

Transition is also not about going backwards. After all, in many ways we have far better lives today than previous generations did. Transition is forward looking and concerned with the next stage of development in human society. Our hope is that we can learn from the past and combine it with the best of today to create a better future.

And Transition is not all doom and gloom. Recognising that we are facing huge challenges should not be a cause for pessimism. We believe in humanity and know that we have the capacity to make the necessary changes that these challenges will force upon us. There are numerous examples from other transition initiatives around the world showing that changes they have already made have been for the best and helped create stronger communities and happier, healthier individuals.

The Transition Movement provides a framework for people to come together and work with other local organisations to help their communities become more resilient to peak oil, climate change, economic crises and other fundamental challenges.

Transition Penwith is actually the second oldest Transition group in the world (after the original Transition Town, Totnes in Devon), and is linked to other Cornish Transition Town groups and Transition Cornwall Network. We were set up by local people and our members are all of you reading this: concerned citizens and local community and environmental groups. We recognise that we may not have all the right answers but that by working together we may at least start with the right questions!

At its core, Transition is about recognising there is a need to "get real" and accept that the lifestyles we now have are completely underpinned by plentiful oil supplies. Because these supplies are finite scarcity will result and this is likely to lead to dramatic price rises.

Peak oil

Oil has a key role in almost every manufacturing sector: plastics, fertilisers, pharmaceuticals and many other not so obvious industries. Plentiful oil also makes transport relatively cheap, and while transport is cheap the whole economy is distorted.

For example, for the supermarkets and other large shopping chains it is cheaper and more "efficient" to buy from the major suppliers, bring the products into huge centralised warehouses, and then truck them out to their stores. The result is that many local independent shops, producers and suppliers go out of business because they are unable to compete with the false cheapness of the chain stores. And the price you pay for products in many of the major chains is falsely low: products are made in sweat shops overseas or British producers are forced to lower their prices almost to the point of bankruptcy. The true costs – the hidden environmental and social costs – are still there but they are passed on to our children and grandchildren.

Many people regard this as something inevitable – the price of progress. We disagree.

In reality it is plentiful supplies of cheap oil that have made the world the way it is. What would happen if that cheap oil was no longer available? For a start, large scale and apparently efficient distribution systems would no longer be financially viable and the supermarket and warehouse shelves would rapidly empty.

Of course there are still vast untapped reserves of oil. But they are in more and more inaccessible places and the oil is harder – and therefore more expensive – to extract. Many energy analysts agree that we are approaching the peak in oil discovery; the majority think that we have already passed it. Whether we have passed peak oil discovery already or whether it will be in the next few years, peaks in production and consumption will follow shortly afterwards. After that the oil supply will decline, pushing up prices higher and higher, and inevitably consumption will have to decline as well.

This situation is made worse as it is happening at a time when international demand – particularly in the developing world – is rising, and rising, and rising... The difference between demand and supply will only expand. Unless, we do something about it; unless we transition.

Many optimists say (correctly) that the oil supply will not dry up overnight. But they then assume (wrongly) that we can delay any adaptation until serious supply problems have already begun. The position of the Transition Movement, however, is that if we want to make a "smooth transition" to a civilisation that is not reliant on oil then we need to begin now, while oil is still relatively plentiful. If we fail to do this, then someday soon we may face a "precipice transition" induced by erratic increases in price and erratic decreases in supply of oil. These are likely to have a dramatic effect on the functioning of our society and we should not pretend otherwise. Falling off a cliff into a swamp is never pleasant!

Climate change

There is, however, another challenge that might make a smooth transition more difficult to achieve: climate change.

Put simply, human activity is creating an increased concentration of greenhouse gasses in the earth's atmosphere, particularly carbon dioxide (CO_2) from fossil fuel use. As this stops more and more of the sun's energy being radiated back into space, there is likely to be a global average temperature increase of between 2 and 4°C, or even as high as 6°C, by the end of the century (relative to 1980-99 levels).

As the oceans absorb more of this heat, seawater expands and causes a rise in sea levels. Once the full effects of glacial and ice sheet melting are also taken into account, there could be significant rises in average sea levels by the end of the century.

Discussion of climate change often tends to focus on these averages of global temperature increase and rise in sea level, but there will be significant regional variations, and many of the most damaging consequences will be

7

associated with the extremes, and with altered weather patterns in particular. This will have obvious implications for disease patterns and human health, as well as impacting on the types of the crops we are able to grow in different locations.

Let us be absolutely clear: climate change is real, it is almost certainly caused by human activity, and it could have devastating consequences. The overwhelming majority of scientific evidence supports the existence of human-induced climate change. Those that disagree with this are on the margins but are often amplified by well-organised lobby groups funded by the major oil companies and given an unwarranted platform in the right-wing and tabloid press.

The scientific debate has long moved beyond whether climate change is happening or not and what the likely causes might be – all serious debate is now focussed on how to prevent, mitigate and adapt. And this is what Transition is about.

Economy

Research by the HM Treasury found that if the more dramatic predictions come to pass, then inaction on climate change could cost the world economy more than 20% of global GDP each year (whereas the costs of effective action could be limited to just 1% of global GDP each year).

Our economy is already struggling, particularly since the global economic crisis that began in 2008. This latest crisis has revealed our economy's fundamental flaws: it is built on debt and oil. It is a house of cards. So we already need to develop and adopt new ways of working, spending and saving. Once we take into account peak oil and climate change the need to develop new systems should surely be obvious. The emperor has no clothes!

Some people argue that we will learn to live with the situation when the time comes: our communities will adapt and new technologies will be developed and we will manage. Previous generations, after all, managed on a lot less and also had to respond to global challenges such as wars and pandemics.

This faith in the human spirit and our wonderful ability to adapt also lies at the heart of Transition. But we do not allow it to blind us to what is happening in the world and our optimism does not lead us to believe in a "business as usual" approach.

Previous generations had far lower material aspirations than are currently prevalent and promoted. People today, in contrast, have huge material expectations and what are really luxuries are often viewed as necessities ("but I need the new iPhone!"). Previous generations were also more likely to live in self-sustaining communities – villages with a butcher, baker and candlestick maker (or at least a blacksmith!) – and have learned many useful skills from their parents and grandparents. Today we have become so "educated" and specialised that many of our jobs would be useless in a post-oil world: we might be able to develop a social media strategy for launching a new internet start-up in an emerging market, for example, but would not have the first clue how to grow enough food to feed our family for a year.

So if everything did go pear-shaped tomorrow we would not only have fallen off a cliff into a swamp but it would be a swamp full of exceedingly angry and desperate people! If we do not want this kind of society in the future then we must accept that everyone needs to start doing things differently in the here and now, while the transition is easier.

Precipice transition

Good physical infrastructure and social services bring the risks of untimely death and suffering down to acceptable levels. In the developed world, infrastructure is both universal and near invisible. Electricity comes from distant generating stations and is carried over the national grid to our homes. Drinking water is stored in huge reservoirs, treated with chemicals and piped direct to homes. Waste solids and liquids are carried away from our homes over a separate system of sewer pipes using yet more fresh water. There are also gas distribution pipes, storm water drains, roads, railways and the infrastructure of telecommunications.

Infrastructure is, in itself, a public health system and – even with plentiful and cheap oil – it is very expensive. The result is that it needs large organisations to raise the capital required to construct the system and a long period of stable use to pay for it. The developed world has harnessed science, technology, engineering, law, finance, a large and sophisticated manufacturing base, skilled workers and many other systems to produce effective services at a viable price.

Ownership arrangements are often incredibly complex and there are a number of common layers of infrastructure ownership: individual... household... neighbourhood (village, town or city)... region... country... international. Above the household layer infrastructure systems often have very conflicted relationships between the various parties involved in ownership and usage. These large-scale organisations are exactly the kinds of structures that do not thrive in unstable times. And yet, ironically, infrastructure failure or collapse at a time of crisis can often result in a situation that is more dangerous than the original disaster.

Imagine a serious flu epidemic. The 1918 Spanish Flu pandemic killed more people than World War I, but we wouldn't need our imagined epidemic to actually kill people, just disable huge numbers of people for a few days. There would be many, many problems but perhaps the most acute would be that thousands of lorry drivers would not, physically, be able to carry out deliveries of food and other essentials – either because of their own ill-health or knock-on effects from the ill-health of others. The usual saviours of last resort – the armed forces – would be just as affected. So – at the end of the day – in Penwith we could be on our own.

This kind of scenario highlights the sheer brittleness of our long-distance, just-in-time systems. We are consuming more goods than ever before but they are all coming from far away and are a hair's breadth away from not being delivered. There is little redundancy in the system and most of us are completely unaware of any other options.

This kind of "precipice transition" – to a future that we might prefer not to experience – might be caused by a pandemic but it could also be triggered by many other sorts of things: financial meltdown, extreme weather – anything that brings about a sudden change and reveals the weaknesses of our long-distance distribution systems.

Would it not be better to start creating a "different kind of business as usual" now rather than trying desperately to maintain the "business as usual" that we currently know?

Smooth transition

The Transition Movement argues that this different kind of business as usual should feature more local patterns of production and distribution and more community supported patterns of ownership and control.

Small-scale, local systems often have much simpler financial, administrative and organisational models. This makes it easier for them to function in a crisis situation. Of course, in our imagined flu pandemic a lot of local people would be incapacitated, but there would at least be a greater "granularity". It would be a case of the many being dependent on the many (some of whom would not be ill) rather than the many being dependent on the few (with a far higher likelihood of the system breaking down).

So doing things locally and together with others in our communities is probably the most important tool that we have in dealing with whatever comes our way as a result of the insecurities in energy, climate and economy outlined above.

Ironically, though, near neighbours often do not figure very highly in our social networks these days. The internet means that people are able to connect with "friends" all over the planet but often do not know their next-door neighbour half as well as those they have only ever met online. Of course, when people lived in the same place all their lives people knew their neighbours rather too well and often in a not very nice way: there could be a level of curtain-twitching and gossip which we would find repugnant today.

So once again, we see that Transition thinking is about moving forward rather than looking back. We desperately need to rebuild local communities but we do not want them to be insular and inward-looking in the way that they so often used to be. Diversity is hugely important: not only does it make for a more interesting world but a community's strength comes from the differences between the people involved as well as the similarities.

There also needs to be communication between communities, and there definitely is a role for the internet here.

The internet is a paradoxical creation. To some it is "the work of the Devil" and, admittedly, it does need continuous supplies of electricity and infrastructure maintenance. Others recognise that it is a means of communication and access to knowledge that uses a tiny fraction of the energy that is required to physically move people around or to create printed materials and transport them to the people that need them.

If we were making a planned "smooth transition" to the kind of world that would be both sustainable and pleasant then the internet would almost certainly be part of the plan. Communication via the internet would both facilitate the spreading of new knowledge and act as an "anti-insularity" counter to greater localisation. In fact, it could be so important that here in Penwith we might have to become the guardians of the transatlantic fibre-optic cable that lands at Sennen – ensuring that this important communication route between the continents continued to function.

In the event of a precipice transition, of course, the internet is likely to become an extremely unreliable communication tool. It may have its origins as a network built to withstand a nuclear attack but that was for communications between a very small number of people (mostly US army generals and policymakers) all residing in bunkers with reasonably secure energy supplies. The internet that we all use today has a much finer mesh and our end of the system is likely to get frozen out at an early stage. This is a great shame because it would be during such a period that it would be at its most useful.

So getting to know your neighbours is as important as ever – but not just for the obvious reasons. Doing things with others is important as you are building up social connections which may lead to something bigger in a smooth transition scenario and stronger bonds with others that may get you all through the crunch point of a precipice transition.

This is not the survivalist nonsense of grabbing your gun and heading for the hills. It is about community building, which means taking responsibility for yourself and your actions but also, if required, being on hand to support those that need help. This makes the whole community more resilient.

Living in Penwith, at the end of all the distribution lines, we may be particularly vulnerable in an uncertain future. But our geographical isolation also provides a unique context for building up community resilience. The more people who have anticipated that there might be problems and thought through how they will react and what skills they will need to learn then the better we will all cope if and when the time comes.

Money, money, money

Actions that may seem consistent with bringing about a more sustainable civilisation can sometimes cost more money and this is often money that people simply do not have. Even really positive things that may also save money in the long-term are likely to require, what can seem, an impossibly large financial investment today.

For example, today it may seem that the payback periods for renewable energy installations are quite long. But when oil prices really start going up there will be a knock-on effect to all energy prices and payback times will shrink rapidly. Plus if you are getting your energy from local renewables you will know where you stand – whereas people dependent on the wider grid are likely to experience erratic supply as well as ever-increasing cost.

If, like most people, your finances are limited then it has to become more a matter of spending what money you have in a mindful way. The temptation is to go for getting maximum bang for your bucks as the only criterion and of course this plays right into the hands of the big corporations whose monopolistic position means that they are the only ones who can offer goods at rock-bottom prices. So you might try to reconfigure this in your head. Yes, you want value for your money but perhaps not just financial value. You might want your money to go to things which will also contribute to the community and long term sustainability. Even tiny additions to the financial turnover of small organisations can decide whether they survive and thrive or falter and collapse. So, as far as you are capable, try to boost the financial turnover of the things you want to see more of. See if you can buy local when you can in order to counter the prevailing economic force which is forever sucking wealth away from the periphery and towards the centre. Participation in local exchange trading and local currency schemes can help with this.

It is also very important to realise that this is not about living some kind of "pure" life. Transition Penwith does not want you to be filled with guilt for going on a frivolous car journey; taking your kids to McDonalds; or not having bought organic vegetables. There is no such thing as "transitional correctness" ... for most of us it's more a matter of making the least worst purchasing decision. It's the conscious making of the decision that's the important bit because that's much better than living a whole life of impulse buying triggered by overt and covert advertising or peer group pressure!

The directory

This book is a handbook-cum-directory. We want to flag up the issues described above to locals so that if or when they come to pass people are not as shocked as they might have been and have the potential to embrace their new lifestyles more positively. We are saying: this is how it may well be; and asking: if it actually happens how can we make the best of it?

We want to challenge that little voice that says: "It's not worth me doing anything because it won't have any impact". This book offers some things that you can easily do and buying options that you can easily take in the here and now. If lots more people take those kinds of options then the cumulative effect can be substantial and a smooth transition can be possible. The creation of a civilisation that is genuinely sustainable is, after all, in *everybody's* interest regardless of their current level of wealth, status, educational achievements or whatever.

We have tried to present people or organisations that are doing things in Penwith as well as organisations from further afield that could be supportive, some of which might be replicated in this area in due course. We are also hoping that later editions of this book will have a handbook aspect containing very localised information, some of which might come in very useful if things stopped working suddenly.

Our biggest hope is that Transition Penwith and this book will contribute to the building of social capital: the feeling that "we're all in this together" rather than "I'm all alone". High levels of social capital will help us deal better with both possible transition scenarios. Accrued social capital is what will really assist survival in a precipice transition and this can be built up over years previously, often by working with others on long-term smooth transition projects.

Much of this information is also available for free on the Transition Penwith website:

www.transitionpenwith.org.uk

As already highlighted, the internet can be a strong part of a smooth transition scenario but its usefulness is likely to be limited if a precipice transition comes about. In that eventuality you might be really glad to have this printed book available.

Many people have contributed to and helped make this book a reality. Any mistakes, though, are of course our own. If we have missed an important local resource, then it is an oversight we will correct on the website and in future editions of this book. We welcome additional listings and ideas that might also be incorporated into future updates.

Happy reading!

The Transition Penwith Team

Please make us aware of errors, omissions and outdated information as soon as you can

info@transitionpenwith.org.uk

Transition Penwith
care of the Penwith Centre,
Parade Street
Penzance TR18 4BU
(mailing address only)

Introduction

Arts and Culture

So why do we begin our directory with Arts and Culture? The reason is that the arts can often bring people together more easily than other fields. Shared cultural experiences can have a very profound effect on people and in a short space of time make them feel a strong sense of belonging. Penwith has a rich arts culture in which professional artists and community initiatives often work together hand in hand. Town and village festivals mark the passing of the seasons with carnival arts, home grown music, dance and theatre. The area is also famous for having numerous wonderful artists and sculptors whose work can be seen in the many local galleries. Their skill is, perhaps, to express the spirit of the place and to celebrate the local. In this directory we have decided to concentrate on the festivals happening across the region, listing opportunities to join in with local music making, including choirs and bands. Our criteria have been that activities featured should be community minded and have a low carbon footprint – hence we've concentrated on acoustic music and village hall theatre. We hope this section will grow in future to be truly representative of the very wide range of visual art, performance and cultural activities on offer. Activities we would like to feature alongside the present entries include: galleries, folk and open mike sessions, community organised events – from seasonal celebrations to family fun days, youth arts, concerts and dance in the community. Our aim is to concentrate on the contribution that the arts can make to a smooth transition towards a more sustainable existence. If you have ideas for events that could be included get a head start and contact us so that we can add details to our online directory straight away.

BRASS AND SILVER BANDS

Hayle
- Heyl Town Band
  http://www.hayletownband.co.uk
  Angie May, 07866 570913
  angiemay_uk@yahoo.co.uk

Pendeen
- Pendeen Silver Band
  http://pendeenband.co.uk
  c/o 15 South Place Gardens, St Just, Penzance TR19 7JU
  01736 785846

Penzance
- Penzance Silver Band
  The Band Room, Bread Street, Penzance
  01736 366635

CARN TO COVE - VILLAGE HALL VENUES

Cornwall's performing arts scheme for rural communities filling local halls with poetry, music and drama, stories and dancing each spring and autumn. Local people run the

events and choose the live shows they want to see and hear. Carn to Cove are able to offer subsidised tickets at £2 each for group bookings of young people in the spring season of 2012. If you are involved in a school or youth group please give them a call to book.

Web: **http://www.carntocove.co.uk**

Email: **admin@actcornwall.org.uk**

Phone: **01209 313 200**

Address: **Cornwall Arts Centre Trust Ltd,
Krowji, West Park, Redruth, Cornwall TR15 3AJ**

Carn to Cove use the following village hall venues in Penwith:

Carleen
- Carleen Village Hall, near Helston TR13 9QR, 01736 763457

Leedstown
- Leedstown Village Hall, near Hayle, TR27 5XX, 01736 758451

Lelant
- Lelant Village Hall TR26 3JR, 01736 758451

Nancledra
- Towednack and Nancledra Community Hall, Nancledra, Penzance, TR20 8NR, 01736 794711

Newlyn
- The Centre, Chywoone Hill, Newlyn TR18 5AR 01736 365890

Penzance
- The Acorn, Parade Street, Penzance TR18 4BU
  http://www.theacornpenzance.com
  01736 363545
- Mounts Bay Academy, Boscathnoe Ln, Heamoor TR18 3JT 01736 363240

Praa Sands
- Praa Sands and District Community Centre, Pengersick Lane, Praa Sands, Penzance TR20 9SL, 01736 763102

St Just
- Cape Cornwall School, St Just TR19 7JX, 01736 788501

Sancreed
- Sancreed Village Hall, Rosmerrin, Bosvenning, Newbridge, Penzance TR20 8QN, 01736 788705

OTHER VENUES

Penzance
- Exchange Gallery, Princes Street, Penzance TR18 2NL

 VENUES

Sennen
- Sennen Churchtown Hall, Sennen TR19 7AX
  http://sennenvillagehall.weebly.com

St Just
- Plen-an-Gwarry, St Just TR19 7LS
  The oldest working outdoor ampitheatre in Britain.
  Mary Ann Bloomfield, 07966 862559, info@plenproject.com
- St Just Town Hall
  Large performance space available to hire for Community events.
  01736 788357, info@stjustcommunityhall.org.uk
- Bosavern Community Farm, St Just
  Community Celebrations, regular singing group, performance, workshops and family fun. To find out about the next event see:
  www.bosaverncommunityfarm.org.uk

Arts and Culture

COMMUNITY CHOIRS AND SINGING GROUPS

Carbis Bay

- St Ives and Hayle Afternoon Community Choir (part of Cornwall Community Choirs)
Tuesday afternoons, 2.00pm to 3.30pm. £3 per session.
St Anta's Church Hall, Porthrepta Road, Carbis Bay TR26 2LB
Neil Shepherd, 07950 585787 or 01736 759944

Hayle

- Local Vocalz (part of Cornwall Community Choirs)
http://www.localvocalz.co.uk
Monday evenings 8.00pm – 9.30pm
Passmore Edwards Institute, Hayle
Fast moving, young choir of approximately 70 people. Music reading desirable, but not essential if you are prepared to have a go at picking up simple music reading skills fairly quickly. Regular concerts, recordings, and trips. This choir is aimed at people in the 18 to 50 age range although those outside that range are welcome. Repertoire: classical, madrigals, jazz, pop show tunes. £3 per session.
Neil Shepherd, 07950 585787 or 01736 759944

Helston

- Helston Community Choir (part of Cornwall Community Choirs)
Mondays from 1.30pm to 3.00pm. £3 per session.
Catholic Church Hall, Clodgey Lane, Helston
07950 585787 or 01736 759944

Marazion

- Apollo Male Voice Choir
http://www.apollo-choir.co.uk
Musical Director: Timothy Hosken
01736 810349, timhosken@hotmail.co.uk

Mousehole and Paul

- Mousehole Male Voice Choir
http://www.mouseholemalevoicechoir.co.uk
Monday Evenings 7:30 – 9:15pm
Mousehole Sunday School Room (November to April); Paul Parish Church (May to October). Choir members are drawn from all over west Cornwall, and are a cosmopolitan group, representing many backgrounds, from labourers to head teachers, high flying council employees to painters and decorators, and aged from

22 to 88. This is a varied group of well over 80 men, who come together as equals. Teamwork is a key with the men working hard to extend and improve on their repertoire, the committee working to make events and ideas come to fruition, and balance the books, and the music team leading from the front. If you're interested in joining the choir you are very welcome to visit on a practice night. Musical Director: Steven Lawry.
Tim James, 01736 361371, mmvc@talktalk.net

Newlyn

- Newlyn Male Voice Choir
  http://newlynmalechoir.co.uk
  Monday Evenings 7.30pm – 9.30pm
  The Trinity Centre, Paul Hill, Newlyn
  If you are interested go and sit in one evening. Being able to read music is not a necessity.
  info@newlynmalechoir.co.uk

Paul

- Laudate!
  Paul Parish Church, http://www.laudatechoir.co.uk
  Mixed voice four part choir, open to singers who would like to sing a wide range of "quality" music from Tallis to Tavener and a multiplicity of other composers. Singers drawn from Lands End to Truro undertaking a variety of engagements, including services, concerts and recitals. Choir specialises in church music but also performs concerts with a broader repertoire. £3/session.
  Neil Shepherd, 07950 585787 or 01736 759944

Penzance

- Barbed Choir
  www.thefiftydegrees.moonfruit.com/#/barbed-choir/4553986401
  Thursday evenings 7.00pm - 8.30pm
  Humphry Davy School, Penzance
  Barbed Choir sing arrangements of songs by the likes of Adele, Fleet Foxes, Mumford & Sons and even Britney Spears! Songs are learnt by ear so no need to read music. No audition needed, everybody is welcome.
  Craig, 07584 043646; Sophie, 07773 330393
- Levow an Bys (Voices of the World)
  http://levowanbys.co.uk
  Wednesday evenings during term-time, 7.00pm - 9.00pm
  The Community Rooms at Humphry Davy School, Penzance
  A friendly community choir which sings beautiful songs from

around the world (in 2, 3 and 4 parts). The choir performs a few times a year – but mostly sing for pleasure, relaxation and the delight of singing in harmony. All voices welcome, men, women ... high, low or 'not sure what I am' voices. No audition and no need to read music. Led by Pip Wright.
01736 763766, pipjanewright@gmail.com

- Penzance Choral Society
  http://www.penzancechoral.org.uk
  7.30pm on Friday evenings at Humphry Davy School, Coombe Road, Penzance. Over 100 voices strong, the choir perform two main concerts a year (May and Christmas) and also sing in local churches at special events. New members always very welcome.Musical Director: Timothy Hosken
  Tim Hosken, 01736 810349, info@penzancechoral.org.uk
- Penzance Community Choir (part of Cornwall Community Choirs)
  Thursday afternoons, 1.30pm to 3.00pm. £3 per session.
  St Mary's Church, Chapel Street, Penzance
  Neil Shepherd, 07950 585787 or 01736 759944

Perranuthnoe
- Perran Voices
  Meet fortnightly on Tuesday afternoons (1.00pm - 3.00pm) Church Room Community Centre, Perranunthoe. £3.50 per session. A friendly local singing group which sings a mixture of beautiful, easy-to-learn songs from around the world (and closer to home). Each session starts with gentle warm ups and vocal technique to help singers find their voice, gain confidence and sing healthily. New voices are always welcome, the group is a mixture of men, women, different ages and with varied singing backgrounds. There is no pressure to perform or attend every session. Led by Pip Wright.
  01736 763766, pipjanewright@gmail.com

St Just
- Cape Cornwall Singers (Male Voice Choir)
  http://www.capecornwallsingers.co.uk
  Formed early in 1997 in an attempt to resurrect the singing tradition in the local pubs around St Just.
  01736 787120
- Bosavern Singers
  Bosavern Community Farm
  Alternate Sundays 4pm to 5.30pm. £2 per session. Singing is inside or outside depending on the weather. Members of the

group bring material they would like to sing and the repertoire is varied. A focus has been to find songs to mark the seasons, and daily activities on the farm. Sessions are led by Kelsey Michael.
01736 351330

Cornwall Community Choirs
http://www.cornwallcommunitychoir.co.uk
Musical Director of choirs: Neil Shepherd
The aim is to get people singing in a network of community based choirs throughout the county. There are five daytime groups. All Community Choirs: £3.00 per session.
neilshepherd@yahoo.co.uk

FESTIVALS

FEBRUARY

St Ives, Monday after February 3

FESTIVALS

• St Ives Feast
  A celebration of the founding of
  St Ives by St Ia. It includes a civic procession to Venton Ia, the well of St Ia, and other associated activities. It is most notable as one of the two surviving examples of Cornish Hurling.

MARCH

Penzance, March 5

• St Pirans Day
  St Piran was the patron saint of Tin Miners and this day started as one of the many tinners' holidays observed by miners. Features the annual performance of the St Piran Furry Dance and a procession through the streets by hundreds of children.

St Just, April 30

• Beltane Celebration
  Welcoming in the May with music and dancing around the maypole at Bosavern Community Farm.

MAY

Penzance, nearest Sunday to May 1

• Mayhorns
  http://www.cornishculture.co.uk/mayhorns.htm
  Celebration of the coming of May and summer.

Helston, May 8
- Flora Day
  http://www.helstonfloraday.org.uk
  This celebration is believed to be pre-Christian and at one time during the Victorian era was banned as being "a drunken revelry." The whole town is decorated with local greenery and bluebells from the surrounding countryside. The day starts with the 7am dance (originally for the servants of the gentry) with the gentlemen wearing shirt and tie and the ladies wearing light summer dresses. This is followed by a boisterous dance cum play called the Hal-an-Tow. Dances and celebrations follow throughout the day.

SPRING OR EARLY SUMMER

St Michael's Mount, annually for a single day
- Music on the Mount
  http://www.stmichaelsmount.co.uk
  Free entry to the Castle, Gardens and live music and entertainment

JUNE

Penzance, week including June 24 (2012 dates: June 14 to 24)
- Golowan Festival
  http://www.golowan.org
  A week of entertainment and celebrations including the election of a new Mock Mayor, fireworks on Mazey Eve, community processions on Mazey Day on Saturday, and Quay Fair Day on the Sunday. Golowan was one of the last mid summer festivals practiced in Cornwall and was outlawed due to the rising insurance premiums! Traditionally blazing tar barrels were paraded around the town's streets and the surrounding hills had bonfires set at the top. The midsummer Feast of Saint John (Gol–Jowan) was revived in 1991. It has now become the most colourful community festival in the South West – totally unique, nationally and internationally, but never losing its sense of tradition and place, blending Cornish tradition with contemporary imagery and ritual.

Resilient Penwith 2012

JULY

Mousehole, long weekend in July in even numbered years (2012 dates: July 6 to 8)

- Sea Salts and Sail
  http://www.seasalts.co.uk
  Traditional sailing boats racing in Mounts Bay; live music; delicious food and drink; cookery demonstrations; demonstrations of local crafts; photographic display of Old Cornwall.

St Just, Lafrowda Day is third Saturday in July preceded by a week or two of events (2012 dates: July 13 to 21)

- Lafrowda Festival
  http://www.lafrowda-festival.co.uk
  Lafrowda is the ancient name for the church lands where St Just in Penwith stands today. The modern festival first took place in 1996. It offers community events plus a festival workshop programme. The culmination of the festival is Lafrowda Day when roads are closed and decorations go up. From hip hop to harmony, from folk to funk, twelve hours of free entertainment to suit every taste plus three spectacular processions. All this and street performers, stalls, refreshments, bouncy castles and a great family-friendly atmosphere.

Marazion, a Sunday in July (2012 date: July 15)

- Marazion Carnival
  Free fun and entertainment. Live music, dancers, magic, Punch & Judy, demonstrations, games, a tug-of-war competition, a barbeque, cream teas and lots of stalls as well as a noisy and colourful procession.

Penzance, four days at the end of July (2012 dates: July 25 to 29)

- Penzance Literary Festival
  http://penzance-literary-festival.org.uk
  A festival about the written word, the spoken word, the recited word and the sung word too. Talks by authors and people with a deep knowledge of subjects special to West Cornwall. Round table discussions, authors in conversation, and workshops on writing, poetry and drama. Performance and entertainment in the evenings.

AUGUST

Morvah, first Tuesday in August (2012 date: August 7)

- Morvah Pasty Day
  http://www.morvah.com
  Day starts with food, live music (folk), children's activities, a car boot sale, as well as stalls within a marquee and ... pasties. On into the evening with more music and a bar with a selection of Real Cornish Ales!

Resilient Penwith 2012

Goldsithney, Saturday closest to August 5 (2012 date: August 4)
- Goldsithney Charter Fair
  http://www.goldsithneycharterfair.org
  Processions, stalls, Cornish Wrestling, live music, street theatre.

Penzance, August Bank Holiday Sunday (2012 date: August 26)
- Party in the Park
  http://www.trereifepark.co.uk
  An annual music event which is all about the best local bands playing under cover in marquees within the grounds of Trereife Park, west of Penzance on the A30.

Newlyn, August Bank Holiday Monday (2012 date: August 27)
- Newlyn Fish Festival
  http://www.newlynfishfestival.org.uk
  Satisfy your appetite with the best seafood you can get whilst enjoying great cooking demos, live entertainment or bidding at the seafood auction. (2012: 9am to 5pm, admission £5.)

Sennen, some August Bank Holiday Mondays
- End of the Road Show

SEPTEMBER

Botallack, a Sunday early in September
- Botallack Country Fair
  Vintage vehicles, traction engines, tin smelting, granite splitting, tin panning, blacksmithing, withy crafts plus spinning and weaving. Food stalls from local producers, duck wrangling and a sheep dog skills demonstration.

St Ives, 15 day event in mid September (2012 dates: Sep 8 to 22)
- St Ives September Festival
  http://www.stivesseptemberfestival.co.uk
  One of the longest running and widest ranging festivals of the arts in the UK, presenting a range of arts from Music (including Folk, Jazz, Rock, Classical and World) to Poetry, Film, Talks and Books. Free music in many pubs almost every night plus well-attended concerts. (2012 acts include; Kate Rusby, The Blockheads, Billy Bragg, The Beat and Fishermans Friends.)

DECEMBER

Penzance, December 21
- Montol Festival
  http://www.montol.co.uk

Montol is a festival of revived local traditions of midwinter. People come in disguise, masks and costume, tatters or mock formal, carrying a lantern, wending their way to the ancient Lescudjack Hillfort, and the lighting of the great beacon to celebrate the coming of the light on the darkest day of the year.

Mousehole, December 23

- Tom Bawcocks Eve
  The festival is held in celebration and memory of the efforts of Mousehole fisherman Tom Bawcock to lift a famine from the village. Star Gazey Pie – a mixed fish, egg and potato pie with protruding fish heads – is eaten.

PERFORMING COMPANIES

- Bash Street Theatre Company
  http://www.bashstreet.co.uk
  Outdoor shows suitable for all.
  Indoor rural touring shows. Stilt walking. Shows are Inspired by the silent movies of Buster Keaton and Charlie Chaplin often featuring daring stunts.
  35 Belgravia Street, Penzance, Cornwall TR18 2BL
  01736 360795, office@bashstreet.co.uk
- Family Album Theatre Company
  A new theatre company based in Penzance, working towards a sustainable approach to making magical, high quality performance work. In their first work Dusk to Dark, a small theatre in the landscape frames the dusk, capturing twilight adventures in music and light on a campsite somewhere deep in Cornwall. The show is aimed at Village Hall Fields, festivals, as well as seeking to discover new venues such as farms and campsites.
  01736 351330
  minnowsoftshoe@googlemail.com
- Shallal Dance Theatre
  http://www.shallal.org.uk
  A dynamic, celebratory, socially inclusive company which engages, explores and integrates improvised dance theatre, providing a performance space for anyone in the community, regardless of sexuality, gender, race, age, physical, mental, and emotional status. Shallal seeks to enable artistic expression, improve physical health and self–confidence and provide an

experience that will enhance the quality of life for all members through professionalism, dedication, skill acquisition and sheer good fun.
c/o The Penwith Centre, Parade Street, Penzance TR18 4BU
07856 426150, admin@shallal.org.uk
* Squashbox Theatre
http://www.squashboxtheatre.co.uk
Craig Johnson of Squashbox produces quality performances involving puppetry, storytelling, live music and comedy for schools, theatres, village halls, festivals and events. Current shows include; The Sea Show and Skillywidden (recommended for ages 5-11) and Universarama! (for adults and children aged 7+).
07769 646345 or 01736 741123

THE TRE PROJECT

Tre is the Cornish word for 'Home' or 'Homestead'. Using archive film as its inspiration and 'home' as its theme, the Tre Project collects old cine footage, creates digital content and produces a programme of new

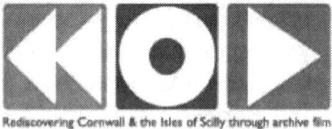

THE TRE PROJECT

films to screen in community venues across Cornwall and the Isles of Scilly. The idea is to stimulate interest, debate and get the Cornish community involved in following the story and sharing old films. If you don't have any footage but do have a unique story of Cornwall to share Tre will try to find existing footage that could go with it.

Web: **http://thetreproject.wordpress.com**
Email: **barbara@awen.org.uk**

Building and Housing

In Penwith we have a huge stock of visually charming houses with a large proportion of them based on solid granite wall construction. Many are quite small – nothing wrong with that but it means that if you try to insulate the walls on the inside it makes the rooms even smaller. External insulation can mean that the edge of the wall no longer comes within the existing eaves. And if you overcome that issue then you'll probably find that your house is in a conservation area and you won't be permitted to cover up the stone wall anyway!

It's all insanely difficult but we *must* start addressing this problem because all forms of heating are just going to get more and more expensive. We can't go on pouring those valuable resources into houses that leak heat like sieves. There is good reason for a lot of planning controls but the preoccupation with preserving the olde worlde look of everything is something that is enabled by the luxury of cheap energy. When that is gone we will have other things on our minds and the cute look of our houses will not be amongst them.

As for new build ... many people are amazed to discover that it's not extortionately expensive to construct "zero energy" houses (that keep warm just with sunlight; body heat; and spin-off heat from cooking). Such dwellings need to be south facing; very well insulated and glazed; have heat recovery ventilation systems; and preferably be in terraces. Terraces imply a proximity to neighbours that can also lead to other forms of co-operation – so it's a win-win situation. To make this work in an intentional way some people even set up housing co-ops or cohousing communities. Could such things happen in Penwith?

CORNISH LIME BUILDERS

Specialise in all aspects of granite work; from hedging to openings in listed buildings, new build in 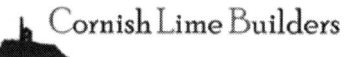 lime to existing structures, scantle roofing and wet laid alternative slate roofs, lime rendering and plastering, lime pointing with a wide variety of colours and finishes, lime grouting which stabilizes old washed out /rat run structures and more. They also use modern materials and techniques and are up to date with the building regs.

Web: http://cornishlimebuilders.co.uk

Phone: 01736 364 882

Address: 28 Leskinnick Terrace, Penzance, Cornwall TR18 2HB

CORNISH LIME COMPANY

Building lime, limewash and paint pigments. The Cornish Lime Company manufacture in Cornwall but use Derbyshire limestone. They  make a completely natural cement, fast setting, called Prompt and sell this all over the country for renovating old buildings. They also make Hemsulate, an insulation made from hemp and a lime binder.

Web: http://www.cornishlime.co.uk

Phone: 01208 797 790

Address: Brims Park, Old Callywith Road,
Bodmin, Cornwall PL31 2DZ

CORNWALL SUSTAINABLE BUILDING TRUST

Cornwall Sustainable Building Trust (CSBT) gives advice, guidance and training in the understanding and skills needed to build sustainably in Cornwall.

Web: http://www.csbt.org.uk

Email: admin@csbt.org.uk

Phone: 01726 64651

Address: Tehidy Cottages, Burngullow Lane,
St Austell, Cornwall PL26 7TQ

JACOBS JOINERY

Provides local properties with locally manufactured bespoke joinery using, preferably, locally sourced material in the most environmentally friendly way - using renewably generated electricity and non-toxic or eco-friendly materials.

Web: **http://www.jacobsjoinery.co.uk**

Email: **adams4cycling@hotmail.com**

Phone: **07816 049 453**

Address: **2 Trevelloe Farm, Lamorna, Penzance TR19 6NX**

MUDDY MORTARS

Muddy Mortars specialise in ecological and traditional building techniques such as lime and clay plastering, newbuild cob, cob repairs, and straw bale construction. They also offer lime pointing, earthen floors and cob ovens, and will run courses on request. They believe that the use of a breathable finish such as lime is essential in maintaining the health of an old building.

Email: **muddymortars@gmail.com**

Phone: **01736 338 986**

Address: **12 Strawberry Fields, Crowlas, Penzance TR20 8BH**

NATUREPAINT

Award-winning Naturepaints are made here in Cornwall, from natural local materials, like genuine Cornish clays. Washable, low-static surfaces. Non-toxic 100% eco-friendly, these paints reduce health risks from condensation and fungal moulds.

Web: **http://www.naturepaint.com**

Phone: **08453 670 140**

Address: **Unit 5, Marsh Lane Industrial Estate, Hayle TR27 5JR**

Building and Housing

OPTIMAL CONSTRUCTION

Optimal Construction has been operating since 1997. They provide general contracting and design and build services to

private clients, architects and the public sector. As a Community Interest Company they now specialise in environmentally beneficial buildings using sustainable materials and methods of fabrication. They also build and advise on sustainable practices for buildings and recreation areas used by the community for the advancement of education. They have a wealth of traditional skills garnered over the last 30 years and are happy to share them before they are forgotten. As general contractors, Optimal is responsible for planning and scheduling the manpower, equipment, materials and subcontractors required for the timely completion of a construction project. They retain a Consulting Engineers practice for use on design and build projects. They also have an in house Architectural Technician. Optimal have made a level one pledge to Future Foundations, the Charter for Sustainable Construction in the South West.

Web: **http://www.optimalconstruction.co.uk**
Email: **optco@aol.com**
Phone: **01209 831 718**
Address: **Keepers Cottage, Clowance Estate, Praze an Beeble, Camborne, Cornwall TR14 0NQ**

SW-ECO WAREHOUSE

SW-Eco Warehouse is committed to driving forward sustainable construction by offering greener building products and services. Their Products section gives you instant access to a range

of selected products with green credentials. The Directory lists companies and retail outlets which specialise in such products and services. Their Advice pages present a range of articles and case studies to inspire and guide you in all that's green and sustainable in the field of building, construction and green living.

Web: http://www.sw-warehouse.co.uk

Email: info@sw-ecowarehouse.co.uk

Phone: 0172 664 651

Address: Tehidy Cottages, Burngullow Lane,
St Austell, Cornwall PL26 7TQ

STUDIOWEST ARCHITECTS

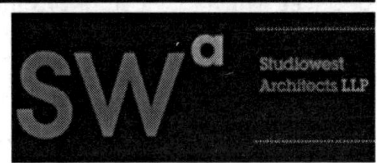

Studiowest Architects is a new practice which continues the works and projects of Arcostudios, Penzance. They specialise in environmentally sustainable architecture and aim to provide the highest quality of design solutions for all types of project, and clients. All of their projects are undertaken with respect for the historical and physical context with a belief that consultation and participation by the users forms an essential part of an effective design process. They have a continually developing focus on energy conservation and sustainability. All of their designs have an ecological bias and the focus of the construction is on craftsmanship, natural materials and energy efficiency

Web: http://www.studiowestarchitects.co.uk

Email: info@studiowestarchitects.co.uk

Phone: 01736 788892

Address: 18 Bank Square, St Just, Penzance TR19 7HJ

TRENOWETH ROOFING AND RECLAMATION

Trenoweth Roofing and Reclamation Services is a small family business based just outside Penzance. In addition to offering various roofing services they sources various reclaimed roofing materials as well as other special items such as chimney pots, clay finials and cast iron sky lights.

Web: http://www.roofingreclamation.co.uk

Email: roofingreclamation@live.co.uk

Phone: 01736 368 292

Address: Ludgvan Leaze, Crowlas, Penzance, Cornwall TR20 8AA

LANDS END PENINSULA COMMUNITY LAND TRUST

Lands End Peninsula Community Land Trust's vision is to provide good quality affordable housing and associated facilities, and resources such as workshops and

Lands End Peninsula Community Land Trust (CLT) Limited

community agriculture, which meet the needs of local people and at prices which they can afford in perpetuity. They aim to sustain a vibrant and diverse community, which is either within or surrounded by Areas of Outstanding Natural Beauty. The principal town is St Just but their area of operation includes all the nearby villages.

Web: http://www.landsendpeninsulaclt.org.uk

Email: info@landsendpeninsulaclt.org.uk

Phone: 01736 788 454

Address: c/o St Just TC, 1 Chapel St, St Just, Penzance TR19 7LS

DIGGERS & DREAMERS

This online directory lists communal groups who live in benders in the woods; in monasteries; in big old country houses; and in newbuild low energy developments. The

Cohousing
in Britain

A Diggers & Dreamers Review

south west is well represented and there are a handful of places in Cornwall ... but sadly none, as yet, in Penwith. Communal living provides an opportunity to live on less with less and to do so in a context that can be much friendlier. D&D's latest book focuses on the theme of cohousing and is an inspirational guide.

Web: http://www.diggersanddreamers.org.uk

UK COHOUSING NETWORK

Cohousing is a form of intentional community where individuals and families have their own self-

the UK COHOUSING NETWORK

contained living units but also have access to many shared facilities as well. It was pioneered in Denmark and the USA more than 20 years ago but is only just getting established in Britain. The UK Cohousing Network is the focus of the movement within this country.

Web: http://cohousing.org.uk

Community
and Local
Government

Community is the hub of everything. We are all members of it but many people perceive the "community" as not something they have much to do with. This attitude is only possible because of cheap energy, it enables us to keep ourselves to ourselves and feel that we can have a life completely independent of others. In times past Penwith would have been an extremely tightly knit community. There would have been good and bad sides to this – too much localism can, after all, lead to insularity and tribalism. And it can be suffocating to have nosy neighbours that are a bit *too* interested ... we don't want to go back to that! But there are worthwhile things that we can do now to make a smooth transition to more pleasant future lives. Increasing energy costs will mean that government and council services will diminish – they just won't be affordable. We need to rebuild neighbourhood support networks so that quality of life does not become intolerable if central services are withdrawn. Number one priority is getting to know your neighbours ... you may feel that you don't have much in common with them now but there may come a time when you will rely on them. Councils and voluntary organisations do many good things but their membership is often drawn from a small part of the population. So get involved in them and help them adapt to the new situation which is unfolding. As ever, there's a silver lining: greater involvement; less resentment; and better capability in dealing with sudden emergencies. And that's something else ... we need to familiarise ourselves with plans for civil contingencies and gain survival skills like first aid and bushcraft just in case a precipice transition leaves us without any central support!

GOVERNMENTAL SYSTEM

HOUSE OF COMMONS	CORNWALL COUNCIL	PARISH/TOWN COUNCILS
Camborne and Redruth Constituency	Hayle North Election District	Hayle Town
	Hayle South Election District	
	Gwinear-Gwithian Election District	Gwinear-Gwithian Parish
St Ives Constituency	St Ives North Election District	St Ives Town
	Lelant and Carbis Bay Election District	
	St Ives South Election District	Towednack Parish
	St Erth Election District	St Erth Parish
	Marazion Election District	St Hilary Parish
		Perranuthnoe Parish
		Marazion Parish
	Ludgvan Election District	Ludgvan Parish
		Zennor Parish
		Madron Parish
	St Buryan Election District	Morvah Parish
		Sancreed Parish
		Paul Parish
		St Buryan Parish
		St Levan Parish
		Sennen Parish
	St Just in Penwith Election District	St Just in Penwith Town
	Newlyn and Mousehole Election District	Penzance Town
	Penzance Central Election District	
	Penzance East Election District	
	Penzance Promenade Election District	
	Gulval and Heamoor Election District	

Resilient Penwith 2012

St Just in Penwith
Sancreed
Morvah
Madron
Zennor
Towednack
St Ives
Hayle
Gwinear-Gwithian
St Erth
St Hilary
Perranuthnoe
Marazion
Ludgvan
Penzance
Paul
St Buryan
St Levan
Sennen

Gwinear Gwithian Parish Council
* http://www.ggpc.org.uk
  01209 614618, vida.perrin@ggpc.org.uk

Hayle Town Council
* http://www.hayletowncouncil.net
  01736 755005, townclerk@hayletowncouncil.net

Ludgvan Parish Council
* 01736 751790, edwr393@aol.com

Madron Parish Council
* http://www.madron.org
  01736 762874, cornerbarn@talktalk.net

Resilient Penwith 2012

Marazion Town Council
- 01736 710234

Morvah Parish Meeting
- 01736 786716

Paul Parish Council
- 01736 811020, paulpc@btinternet.com

Penzance Town Council
- http://www.penzancetowncouncil.co.uk
  01736 363405, townclerk@pz-towncouncil.fsnet.co.uk

Perranuthnoe Parish Council
- http://www.perranuthnoepc.info
  01209 831269, james.jacoby@yahoo.co.uk

Sancreed Parish Council
- 01736 811020, sancreedpc@btinternet.com

Sennen Parish Council
- 01736 811020, sennenpc@btinternet.com

St Buryan Parish Council
- 01736 811020, stburyanpc@btinternet.com

St Erth Parish Council
- 01736 757575, sterthpc@hotmail.co.uk

St Hilary Parish Council
- 01736 763311, roger.calfe@btinternet.com

St Ives Town Council
- http://www.stivestowncouncil.co.uk
  01736 797840, townclerk@stivestowncouncil.co.uk

St Just in Penwith Town Council
- http://www.stjust.org
  01736 788412, townclerk@stjust.org

St Michael's Mount Parish Meeting
- 01736 710507, info@lesleyround.co.uk

Towednack Parish Council
- 01736 740931, towednackpcclerk@usermail.com

Zennor Parish Council
- http://www.zennor.org
  01736 799069, lottie.millard@hotmail.co.uk

Cornwall Council
- http://www.cornwall.gov.uk
  0300 1234 100

CORNWALL COMMUNITY FOUNDATION

CCF is an organisation that aims to improve the lives of others in Cornwall, especially those who are isolated, disadvantaged and vulnerable. They give small grants to grassroots, front line and  volunteer led organisations to make that happen as well as teaming donors and projects together. They are independent and rely on donations to fund them and continue their services.

Web: **http://www.cornwallfoundation.com**
Email: **office@cornwallfoundation.com**
Phone: **01566 779 333**
Address: **Suite 1, Sheers Barton, Lawhitton, Launceston PL15 9NJ**

PENWITH COMMUNITY DEVELOPMENT TRUST

Penwith Community Development Trust is a charitable and not-for-profit organisation which was formally set up in 1999. It aims to work in partnership towards the  economic, environmental and social regeneration of the community. The aims of the PCDT include promoting and developing community economic initiatives of benefit to Cornwall communities; acting in partnership with the Voluntary and Community Sector, Public and Private Sector to achieve 'joined up working'. It provides high quality training and capacity building for voluntary and community organisations leading to education, increased transferable skills and enabling better delivery of local projects. It champions the plight of small voluntary sector organisations in Cornwall. The Penwith Centre is a facility near the heart of Penzance where it is possible to rent rooms, offices or hold meetings.

Web: **http://www.pcdt.org**
Email: **enquiries@pcdt.org.uk**
Phone: **01736 334 686**
Address: **The Penwith Centre, Parade Street, Penzance TR18 4BU**

REAL IDEAS ORGANISATION

Real Ideas Organisation uses social enterprise to create opportunities for young people and adults. From school improvement through sausage making to job creation

through skate ramps. Their consultancy, services and products help the customers and individuals they work with make change happen.

Web: **http://realideas.org**

Email: **info@realideas.org**

Phone: **08458 621 288**

Address: **Devonport Guildhall, Ker Street, Plymouth PL1 4EL**

THE BIG LUNCH

The aim is to get as many people as possible across the whole of the UK to have lunch with their neighbours in a simple act of community, friendship and fun. In 2011 over a million people took

part. A Big Lunch can be anything from a few neighbours getting together in the garden or on the street, to a full blown party with food, music and decoration that stops the traffic. Locally there have been Big Lunches in Penlee Park and Love Lane, Penzance.

Web: **http://www.thebiglunch.com**

Email: **info@thebiglunch.com**

Phone: **0845 850 8181**

THE CO-OPERATIVE MEMBERSHIP

If you have a Co-operative Membership card it doesn't just get you dividend points but also gives you the right to vote for member representatives in the region. Elected members then meet up every month or so. They are there to ensure that the views of the members are reflected and also to make sure that the organisation follows its values and principles in the local community. Committee members work with The Co-operative management and the wider community.

They discuss the performance of The Co-operative businesses in their area, plan member and community activities and help to decide which groups should receive Community Fund grants. Cornwall and Isles of Scilly Area Committee has 12 elected representatives.

Web: **http://www.co-operative.coop/membership**

Email: **membership.sw@co-operative.coop**

Phone: **01884 266 892**

Address: **The Co-operative Membership Department, Limesfield Broad Road, Dulford, Cullompton EX15 2DY**

THE SUSTAINABLE TRUST

Sustrust was formed by and for a group of people including voluntary groups and small businesses working in association with each other to improve the understanding  and implementation of sustainable practices. Building on the principles of Local Agenda 21, recommended at the first Earth Summit they think globally and act locally to conserve natural resources, and effect small changes to our environment.

Web: **http://www.sustrust.co.uk**

Email: **sustrust@aol.com**

Phone: **01209 831 718**

Address: **Keepers Cottage, Clowance Estate, Praze-an-Beeble, Camborne, Cornwall TR14 0NQ**

TRENCROM DOWSERS

Trencrom Dowsers was formed in late 2011. It aims to have a good mix of talks/presentations/discussions on dowsing and closely related subjects,  as well as visits to interesting sites for practical dowsing experience. New members are welcome and can attend two meetings before formally joining the group. New members at a novice level are required to commit to attending a British Society of Dowsers' beginners' course.

Web: **britishdowsers.org**

Email: **mossinthewoods@btopenworld.com**

Phone: **01736 786 506**

HAYLE PIONEERIUM PROJECT

Hayle Pioneerium Project is about creating an enterprise culture. The Pioneerium will be owned and operated by the community and will be a self-sustainable attraction, which benefits locals, businesses and

visitors. As well as creating jobs it will help address the problem that Hayle has – many visitors to West Cornwall stay there but go elsewhere during the day. After enjoying a trip to the Pioneerium, the visitor will stay in the town, enjoying the other attractions on offer, hopefully leading to a knock-on effect for local businesses.

> Web: **http://www.haylepioneerium.co.uk**
> Email: **info@haylepioneerium.co.uk**
> Phone: **01736 754 117**

GREENPEACE CORNWALL

Greenpeace defends the natural world and promotes peace by investigating, exposing

GREENPEACE

and confronting environmental abuse, and championing environmentally responsible solutions. Greenpeace Cornwall mounts public campaigns and varies them around Cornwall to give everyone a chance. Contact them via the national website.

> Web: **http://www.greenpeace.org.uk/groups/cornwall**

PENZANCE SEAFRONT FORUM

Important decisions are being made about the harbour and seafront of Penzance. Many people

Penzance Seafront Forum
Reconnecting Penzance to the Sea

feel that it is the sea that gives Penzance its identity yet the seafront and harbour have been neglected, despite being the key to the economic, cultural and social well being of the town. The Penzance Seafront Forum is a new initiative to enable the community to work together on a future vision for the seafront and harbour.

> Web: **http://penzanceseafront.com**

WEST CORNWALL FRIENDS OF THE EARTH

Friends of the Earth believe that there is a tomorrow and we need to use the planet like there is a tomorrow. This means living within the limits of the natural

world. Everyone gets a fair share. Everyone, everywhere, now and tomorrow, deserves to have a good life. Rules need to be changed so that the economy works for people and the environment.

Web: **http://www.foe.co.uk/groups/westcornwall**

Phone: **01736 366 876**

WEST CORNWALL GREEN PARTY

What if "business as usual" is no longer an option? Unfortunately the majority of political parties are only **West Cornwall Green Party** too keen to keep "business as usual" going and are rarely prepared to even contemplate a different future in which it may actually be impossible to enact their proposals. All credit then to the Green Party which - since its origins in the 1970s - has always espoused views on a radically different level. The Green Party has members on St Ives Town Council and Ludgvan Parish Council and always puts up candidates in Cornwall Council and UK national elections.

Web: **http://westcornwall.greenparty.org.uk**

Email: **tim@timandrewes.com**

Phone: **01736 795 387**

Address: **c/o 15 Street-an-Garrow, St Ives, Cornwall TR26 1SG**

CORNWALL COUNCIL: EMERGENCY MANAGEMENT

Cornwall Council is responsible for: preparing an Emergency and Business Continuity Management Plan; training Council staff and

voluntary agencies to assist in the management response to major incidents; assisting in the development of multi-agency emergency response plans to identified risks; testing plans through multi-agency exercises; providing general advice to local businesses and voluntary organisations about continuity management; and putting in place arrangements to warn and inform the public.

Web: http://www.cornwall.gov.uk/default.aspx?page=7408

Email: emergencymanagement@cornwall.gov.uk

Address: County Hall, Truro, Cornwall TR1 3AY

LOCAL RESILIENCE FORUM

The purpose of the Forum is to ensure effective delivery of duties under the Civil Contingencies Act. It is intended to be a strategic forum, attended by emergency planners and where appropriate, chief officers. There are fascinating documents on their website.

Web: http://www.dcisprepared.org.uk

SW RAYNET: RADIO AMATEURS' EMERGENCY NETWORK

Amateur radio is useful for emergency communications because it does not depend on any infrastructure (eg the electrical power grid or any cabled network).

SOUTH WEST RAYNET

The South West RAYNET Association (or SWRA) represents all RAYNET Groups in the South West of England.

Web: http://swraynet.org.uk

WRVS

WRVS has trained teams of community support volunteers on call 24 hours a day, 365 days a

year to respond to emergencies. In emergencies they set up rest centres providing shelter, refreshments, registration and information. They also provide emergency feeding at the rest centres. They have all the systems in place to organise food supplies on a large scale.

Web: http://www.wrvs.org.uk/how-we-help/community-support

Education

Traditionally education would have been provided by the whole family and the nearby community. It would have taught us how to live in the widest sense: growing our own food, looking after children, making and repairing things. We would have learnt from our parents and grandparents.

Modern education, however, is premised on teaching us a trade or profession in order to earn money to pay others to do those things for us! It leaves us lacking many of the general skills that in past generations would have been taken for granted.

How would you care for your family if the shops were suddenly empty or if no heating fuel was delivered to your house? This might seem an extreme scenario but it takes such an unnerving vision to make us take stock and reassess where we are. Maybe the survival skills of bushcraft, foraging, fire-lighting and first aid are something that everyone should have?

If we want to make a smooth transition to a world where such panic measures are not necessary then the focus in children's education must move towards real world skills to complement the paper qualifications which are currently advocated. There has to be, at least, a greater awareness that a time may come when such qualifications may be of limited use. Adults also need to be reskilled. At least lifelong learning is now seen as something to be applauded. But could that learning be something which would be genuinely useful in making the local community more sustainable rather than the incentive being a salary increase that enables yet more consumption?

BOSWEDDEN HOUSE

Boswedden House provides a tranquil and comfortable environment for workshops, seminars and retreats. It's a place where body, mind and spirit  can relax and renew in a caring atmosphere yet very elemental location. They can house up to 18 en suite and there is additional accommodation nearby. They offer a varied programme of workshops, courses and retreats including music, poetry, voice and body work, retreats, womens workshops, spiritual training and counselling. They offer a place where people can take time away from their busy lives to reflect and find inspiration from the tranquility of the house and the breathtaking scenery around it.

Web: http://www.boswedden.org.uk

Email: relax@boswedden.org.uk

Phone: **01736 788 733**

Address: **Cape Cornwall, St Just, Penzance, Cornwall TR19 7NJ**

BOTREA

Botrea is a working organic farm which offers holiday accommodation in tipis and yurts. Their ultimate aim is to provide  their guests with the opportunity to learn more about the countryside and increase visitors' environmental awareness primarily by getting involved. They sometimes offer courses with themes of: sustainable organic farming and bushcraft-survival skills. Subjects may include bow making, natural dyeing and spinning, willow weaving, flint knapping, green woodworking, bush craft, tipi and yurt construction, yoga and tai chi.

Web: http://www.botrea.co.uk

Email: info@botrea.co.uk

Phone: **01736 788 926**

Address: **Botrea Farm, Newbridge, Penzance, Cornwall TR20 8PP**

EDUCATION OTHERWISE

Although education is compulsory in the UK for children between the ages of five and sixteen, school is   **educatiŏn otherwise™**

not. Many families prefer to educate their children otherwise than at school, and it is their right under UK law to do so. Home educating families do not have to follow the National Curriculum and there is no single 'right' way to educate a child at home. Education Otherwise provides information and resources for home educating families and those considering home education for the first time, including guidance on home education and the law and links to local home education groups across the UK. In Penzance "PZ Home Ed" meet on Monday afternoons for workshops during term-time. You can contact them via the Education Otherwise website.

Web: **http://www.education-otherwise.net**
Phone: **0845 478 6345**
Address: **PO Box 3761, Swindon, Wiltshire SN2 9GT**

FOREST SCHOOL CAMPS

An educational charity and a voluntary organisation. All officers and staff are unpaid volunteers. Importance has always been attached to the experience of boys  **Forest School Camps**

and girls, children and adults, learning to work and play together close to nature. Their education is about discovering for oneself how to do something, rather than being told in the abstract. They remove unnecessary authority and, with due regard for safety and legality, encourage children to take responsibility and to reach their own decisions on small and not-so-small issues. They aim to teach how to live with independence and responsibility; concern and care for oneself, other people and the environment; resourcefulness and self-confidence; tolerance and respect. FSC is determined that all people be treated equally regardless of age, gender, sexual orientation, ethnic origin, religion and disability.

Web: **http://www.fsc.org.uk**
Email: **enquiries@fsc.org.uk**

45

FUTURE TRACKS

Future Tracks is an action research company providing environmental sustainability consultancy and training. They focus on working with clients to provide bespoke  creative, workable and practical solutions to satisfy their needs and generate new income streams from the resources that they have available. Topics covered include: Bushcraft and Wild Camping; Charcoal Production; Coppicing and Coppice Crafts; Green Woodwork; and much more.

Web: **http://www.futuretracks.co.uk**
Email: **info@futuretracks.co.uk**
Phone: **07776 223 337**

GLOBAL BOARDERS

Global Boarders is a multi award winning surf experience company which looks after people and the planet. Their main motivation is to promote behaviour change  towards a sustainable future by facilitating a reconnection with the natural environment as well as transforming clients through surfing. Empowerment to improve personal and collective responsibility achieved through highly structured informal, outdoor, experiential education where they focus on fun and self-development.

Web: **http://globalboarders.com**
Email: **feelgoodsurfing@globalboarders.com**
Phone: **01736 711 404**
Address: **Sterling House, North St, Marazion, Penzance TR17 0EA**

LILI

LILI is a national non-profit organisation whose mission is to help people reduce their impact

low-impact living initiative

on the environment, improve their quality of life, gain new skills, live in a healthier and more satisfying way, have fun and save money. They run courses, provide factsheets, have an online shop ... and much more.

Web: **http://www.lowimpact.org**
Email: **lili@lowimpact.org**
Phone: **01296 714 184**
Address: **Redfield Community, Winslow, Buckingham MK18 3LZ**

PLAN-IT EARTH

Plan-it Earth Education Project in Sancreed specifically aims to address the need for re-skilling (relearning skills that have become, or are in danger of becoming, forgotten) in order to build healthy, vibrant communities in a post-

peak-oil world. Thus they host a variety of workshops and talks for audiences of all ages. Recent activities and workshops have included: Low-impact sustainable building; Textiles and recycled clothing; Permaculture; Sustainable food growing; Behavioural change; Green wood working; Blacksmithing; Conflict Resolution; and Working with the natural cycles and seasons.

Web: **http://www.plan-itearth.org.uk**
Email: **enquiries@plan-itearth.org.uk**
Phone: **01736 810 660**
Address: **Chyena, Sancreed, Penzance, Cornwall TR20 8QS**

SPACE FOR YOU

They offer a semi-structured healing respite week to people who could make use of the

artistic and therapeutic facilities at Sancreed House. In a quiet setting they offer a flexible program of one session per day that is appropriate to different needs. It is a chance to relax and unwind and review current life issues and blocks as well as experience some deep healing and a sense of inner peace. Residential and non-residential sessions range from counselling to dance; from riding to meditation; and from reflexology to foot massage.

> Web: **http://www.spaceforyou.biz**
> Email: **claredyas@madasafish.com**
> Phone: **01736 810 409**
> Address: **Sancreed House, Sancreed, Penzance TR20 8QS**

WOODCRAFT FOLK

The Woodcraft Folk believe in equality and co-operation. Every week thousands of volunteers and young people meet in community venues and a host  of other places to learn about big ideas through fun activities like singing, playing and debating. Their aim is to develop children's self-confidence and build their awareness of society around them. Through their activities, outings and camps they help members understand important issues like the environment, world debt and global conflict. In recent years they have focused on sustainable development. By encouraging children to think, they hope that they will help build a peaceful, fairer world. There are no groups in Penwith but in Helston there are Woodchip (up to 6 years), Elfin (6-9 years), Pioneer (10-12 years) and Venturer (13-15 years) Groups. Contact them via the central organisation.

> Web: **http://www.woodcraft.org.uk**
> Email: **info@woodcraft.org.uk**
> Phone: **020 7703 4173**
> Address: **Units 9/10, 83 Crampton Street, London SE17 3BQ**

Energy

At the moment we can more or less flip a switch and get what we want. The only thing we have to complain about is the price but for most people energy costs are still a manageable proportion of their income. But this is really going to change in the coming years and many more will be seen as living in fuel poverty by today's standards. Unless we make a parallel change in the way we look at things a lot of people are going to be very unhappy. We need to start powering down now. That little voice that says "I can't be bothered" needs to be gagged and we need to see flipping a switch as a choice. A choice to spend energy and therefore a choice to spend money. Some people get very worried about the cost of leaving electrical items on standby. But once you get a bit nerdy and start using an electricity monitor you realise what it is that *really* uses a lot of energy: devices that use heat (eg ovens); devices that move things mechanically (eg washing machines); and devices that use a little but are on a lot of the time (eg refrigerators). Locally, we are rich in sources of renewable energy – Penwith could be energy resilient and possibly exporting energy up the grid. Community owned power generation (already operational elsewhere in Cornwall) needs our support. If we don't start investing in this now then we'll just be kicking ourselves in the future for frittering time and energy away in a period when we had plenty. But let's not kid ourselves that it will produce as much electricity as we currently have access to. We need to get used to rationing ourselves now in order to make what we have go further and to prepare us for a future where there just isn't an infinite supply. And guess what? There's a double benefit because it will also save us money!

49

AEOLUS POWER (WIND-ENERGY) LIMITED

Aeolus Power (Wind-Energy) Ltd is a specialist wind turbine supplier and installer serving farmers, businesses and communities. In August 2010 the company installed  the first Endurance Wind Power 50kW wind turbine in Cornwall. Two of the company's installers have attained "Endurance Wind Power E-Series Installation Supervisor" status and the company offers a full 'from concept' to 'commissioning' and maintenance service. It was involved in the Gorran Community wind project in Cornwall and has a number of 'joint venture' schemes with farmers across the South West. In March 2011 Aeolus Power (Wind-Energy) Limited launched TOPAZ – its Turbine Output Performance AnalyZer allowing turbine owners to see the output of their wind turbine at any time.

Web: **http://www.apwe.co.uk**
Email: **contact@apwe.co.uk**
Phone: **01454 633 323**
Address: **Foxhole Farm, Pilning Street, Pilning, Bristol, BS35 4JJ**

ATLANTIC WINDPOWER

Atlantic Windpower is a locally-based supplier and installer of small wind turbines, including the well-known Proven range of turbines. Run by Dan Ledger, Atlantic Windpower has installed, serviced and repaired turbines ranging from 2.5kW to 15kW, and has built up an extensive base of knowledge and expertise in the small turbine sector. Atlantic can undertake all aspects of a wind turbine project, from initial assessment, through planning and design, to installation, servicing and repair. Being local, Atlantic can offer keener prices and a faster service than firms based further afield.

Web: **http://atlanticwindpower.co.uk**
Email: **dan@atlanticwindpower.co.uk**
Phone: **0785 440 2572**
Address: **Parc an Yorth, Trewellard, Penzance TR19 7UD**

BECO SOLAR (PART OF KIER GROUP PLC)

Beco Solar are one of the UK's longest established designers and installers of Photovoltaic (PV) solar energy systems. With over

20 years experience, they specialise in PV systems for industrial, commercial marine and domestic uses. Manufacturing their own range of controllers and building custom PV power supplies Beco are Project Partners and Distributors for BP Solar, Schuco and Sharp as well as being Distributors for Exide batteries, Rolls batteries and Morningstar regulators. Beco Limited also supply Proven wind turbines through their Cholwell Wind Energy Division.

Web: **http://www.becosolar.com**
Email: **sales@becosolar.com**
Phone: **01803 866 329**
Address: **Tempsford Hall, Sandy, Bedfordshire SG19 2BD**

CAPTURE ENERGY

Capture believe in integrated systems. Drawing on their wealth of experience and qualifications within the renewable energy field they can

guide and support you throughout the process. They can offer advice on a complete range of renewables including solar panels, heat pumps, wind turbines and biomass boilers, without bias towards any particular technology. A site visit is undertaken to ensure that you get the right renewable energy system for your unique situation. They are able to supply a complete range of renewables and specialise in the effective integration of two or more renewable energy technologies. They are members of the Renewable Energy Association and as such conform to the REAL code of conduct.

Web: **http://www.capture-energy.co.uk**
Email: **mail@capture-energy.co.uk**
Phone: **01209 716 861**
Address: **Unit C2, Pool Business Park, Dudnance Lane, Redruth, Cornwall TR15 3QW**

Energy

GEOTHERMAL ENGINEERING LTD

Geothermal Engineering has brought geothermal specialists together with industry partners to develop the first large-scale deep geothermal power plant in the UK at United Downs near Redruth. The project will involve: drilling and testing the deepest on shore wells in the UK (each of the three wells required for the project will be 4.5km deep); the development of a 10MW electric, 55MW thermal geothermal power plant; and the development of a geothermal centre of excellence in conjunction with Exeter University. The project has planning permission to proceed and drilling should start on the site in late 2012. When the United Downs power plant is operational, Geothermal Engineering hope to roll out similar projects across the South West to produce both electricity and renewable heat. The total target production will be 300 MW of electricity and 1GW of renewable heat across all sites within a 25 year timeframe.

GEOTHERMAL ENGINEERING LTD

Web: **http://www.geothermalengineering.co.uk**
Email: **info@geothermalengineering.co.uk**
Phone: **01326 218 955**
Address: **82 Lupus Street, London SW1V 3EL**

GREENTHINKING RENEWABLES LTD

Greenthinking is an independent and ethical business providing wind turbines and environmental advice for homes, businesses, farms, local authorities, architects, schools and colleges. They have specialised experience in all aspects of wind turbines (5 kW - 500 kW) and can provide a full service including site survey, planning, MCS installation and servicing of your wind turbine. They are based in Devon but have an office in Cornwall.

greenthinking

Web: **http://greenthinking.co.uk**
Email: **ian@greenthinking.com**
Phone: **07841 638 293**
Address: **Hemyock, Cullompton, Devon EX15 3PZ**

Energy

HOTPOD

The Hotpod "exothermic oxidizing reactor" is a unique, limited edition multifuel stove, handbuilt by local Cornish/St Ives artist/  blacksmith Daniel Harding. Built from recycled gas cylinders and old VWs they are an exercise in function and form. Hotpod contemporary retro multifuel stove, woodburning stove, stoves and firetools, fire tongs as seen on BBC tv programme "Pay off your mortgage in 2 years".

Web: **http://www.hotpod.co.uk**
Email: **stoked@hotpod.co.uk**
Phone: **01736 797 285**
Address: **PO Box 137, St Ives, Cornwall TR26 2WW**

ICS RENEWABLES SOLUTIONS

ICS is a family run plumbing and heating company covering all areas of Cornwall. Their business is focused primarily on sustainable energy products but they also offer traditional plumbing and heating services. They are committed  to working with the key manufacturers and sourcing the best products on the market. They strive to provide their customers both commercially viable and environmentally friendly solutions. They were the first company in the South West to have been accredited as a Mitsubishi "AEI", Approved Ecodan Installer. Ecodan is an Air Source Heat Pump using the latest technology to provide an advanced heating and hot water system. IcS is not tied to any manufacturer and is therefore able to offer customers completely independent advice.

Web: **http://www.icsplumbing.co.uk**
Email: **iain.wardman@icsplumbing.co.uk**
Phone: **01736 711 230**
Address: **Hellangove Vean, Gulval, Penzance TR20 8XD**

IN BALANCE ENERGY SYSTEMS

Specialist Suppliers, System Designers and Installers of Solar Photovoltaic (PV) Energy Systems. They supply Solar PV Slates,

Solar PV Panels and Free Standing Solar PV Systems. In Balance work with homeowners, small businesses, trade clients and solar manufacturers to supply, design and install Solar Photovoltaic (PV) Energy Systems. Working with clients in the United Kingdom, France, Spain, Belgium, The Netherlands and Germany.

Web: http://inbalance-energy.co.uk

Email: info@inbalance-energy.co.uk

Phone: 0208 581 3003

Address: 5 Nevin House, Bourne Avenue, Hayes, Middlesex UB3 1QU

INDEPENDENT ENERGY

Independent Energy was launched in 2003. They are a small company with a wealth of expertise and experience, operating mainly in Cornwall with very limited overheads. They are not tied to any particular product manufacturer and can give honest and independent advice about all available products. Their aim is to provide a personal and professional service. Matthew Trewhella - one of the directors is also helping train the next generation of renewable energy experts through one-day courses at the Cornwall Sustainable Building Trust and the Renewable Energy degree course at Falmouth.

Web: http://www.solarpanelcornwall.com

Email: matt@inenergy.co.uk

Phone: 01736 740 955

Address: Trenowin Farm, Ludgvan, Penzance, Cornwall TR20 8BL

Energy

NUON RENEWABLES

Nuon Renewables is a renewable energy developer, working across the UK to develop truly sustainable energy projects that deliver social, economic and environmental value. Their core business is focussed on wind energy – they have around 800MW of potential renewable generation in the pipeline or already operational. Their priority is to deliver wind energy projects that support UK policy objectives of diversifying energy supplies to tackle the challenges of climate change and energy security within a sustainable development framework.

Web: **http://www.nuonrenewables.com**

Phone: **01736 330 171**

Address: **Abbey Warehouse, Abbey Slip,
Penzance, Cornwall TR18 4AR**

PLUG INTO THE SUN

Plug Into The Sun are a fully accredited renewable energy installation company based in West Cornwall working throughout all of Cornwall and Devon. They provide a professional service covering advice, quotes, design installation and commissioning of Solar PV installations. They work with individuals, householders, community groups, schools, business, housing associations and local authorities. Plug Into The Sun were established in 2005 and since that time have become a leading installer in the South West region.

Web: **http://www.plugintothesun.co.uk**

Email: **info@plugintothesun.co.uk**

Phone: **0800 496 1494**

Address: **Unit 15, Long Rock Industrial Estate,
Penzance, Cornwall TR20 8HX**

Energy

RENEWABLE ENERGY CO-OPERATIVE

R-ECO, the Renewable Energy Co-operative, is the UK's only employee-owned installer of solar PV systems. They have installed systems on commercial buildings from factories

Renewable Energy Co-operative

to theatres and work with clients on projects ranging from 10kW to 100kW. They actively seek out opportunities to help communities come together to address the issue of fuel poverty and create a better future.

Web: http://www.r-eco.co.uk

Email: info@r-eco.co.uk

Phone: 01872 870 875

Address: Mount Wellington Mine, Chacewater, Truro TR4 8RJ

SOLARCENTURY

Solarcentury is the UK's leading solar energy company, providing solar technology for buildings. Solarcentury's purpose is to make a big difference in the fight against

solarcentury

climate change by reducing CO_2 emissions through the application of solar energy. Founded by Executive Chairman Jeremy Leggett in 1998, Solarcentury is based in London, with operations in the UK, France, Italy and Spain. It has installed solar on more homes in the UK than anyone else; in total over 2000 solar systems, including those on the Eden Project, Vauxhall Cross Bus Terminal and Europe's largest vertical solar facade on the CIS Tower, Manchester.

Web: http://solarcentury.com

Email: marketing@solarcentury.com

Phone: 020 7803 0100

Address: 91-94 Lower Marsh, Waterloo, London SE1 7AB

SOURCE ENERGY

Source Energy have been designing and installing ground source heat pumps and air source heat pumps in

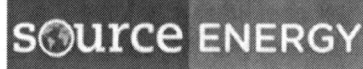

the south west for around a decade. Their installation teams have many

Energy

years of experience in the plumbing and heating industry and they have successfully installed over 250 ground source heat pump and air source heat pump systems across the Cornwall, Devon and Somerset area.

Web: **http://www.sourceenergy.co.uk**

Email: **info@sourceenergy.co.uk**

Phone: **01872 300 201**

Address: **1c Grampound Road Industrial Estate, Grampound Road, Truro, Cornwall TR2 4TB**

SOUTHWEST SOLAR SOLUTIONS

Southwest Solar Solutions specialise in off grid/stand alone renewable energy sytems for **SOUTHWEST SOLAR SOLUTIONS** remote properties where the national grid is prohibitive or non-feasible. They focus on guiding you through the benefits of these power solutions and the use of solar energy as a realistic alternative to conventional power. They can provide clean, reliable solar power on site for your project, from a new build to any outdoor event.

Web: **http://www.southwestsolarsolutions.co.uk**

Email: **fabulousflemings@hotmail.com**

Phone: **01736 850 636**

Address: **Kirthenwood Haven, Bosence Road, Townshend, Hayle, Cornwall TR27 6AJ**

STOVE SHOP RENEWABLES

Stove Shop Renewables is an installer for bespoke renewable energy solutions. With in house, accredited installers, they offer a range of technologies - rainwater harvesting systems, solar thermal, photovoltaic and biomass. They have over 30 years of experience designing bespoke heating systems and are now providing a dedicated installation service that can project manage renewable energy installation from start to finish.

Web: **http://www.stoveshoprenewables.co.uk**

Email: **info@stoveshoprenewables.co.uk**

Phone: **01579 345 018**

Address: **7 Pike Street, Liskeard, Cornwall PL14 3JE**

Energy

SWITCH2SUN

Switch2Sun is owned by Davey & Gilbert Ltd - an established firm of Penzance electrical engineers with experience, knowledge and expertise. They specialise in home  installations of solar photovoltaic panels, a technology that harnesses the sun's energy and converts it into electricity while cutting energy bills. Their installations benefit from a full after-sale service and extensive warranty. They take pride in their installations and will always be on hand to remedy any issues.

Web: **http://www.switch2sun.co.uk**

Email: **info@switch2sun.co.uk**

Phone: **01736 331 133**

Address: **Unit 8a, Long Rock Industrial Est, Penzance TR20 8HX**

COMMUNITY POWER CORNWALL

Community Power Cornwall has evolved through community led demand for the ownership and integration of renewable energy technologies into everyday lives and settings. They hope  to enable local communities to collectively tackle the threats of climate change, energy security and uncontrollable fuel cost rises by generating clean, renewable energy locally involving the whole community in understanding and operations. Community ownership offers the opportunity to create a diverse, sustainable and secure energy supply infrastructure, under control of the community and with profits returned to the local economy. Community Power Cornwall provides an economic model through which Cornish communities can own and benefit from the development of renewable energy initiatives. They are developing a portfolio of renewable energy projects utilising wind, biomass, hydro and solar power. They will develop and operate small to medium scale community owned renewable energy installations with an initial focus on wind turbines generating electricity for sale via the national grid.

Web: http://www.communitypowercornwall.coop
Email: info@communitypowercornwall.coop
Phone: 01209 614 975
Address: 3 Trenhaile Terrace, Malpas, Truro, Cornwall TR1 1SL

GREEN TRUST CIC

Green Trust provides the finance and professional resources required to deliver wind and solar projects from feasibility to operation, and turn a community's visions into reality. Green Trust is managed by experienced renewable energy professionals and supported by experienced suppliers. They will only progress a project that the majority (at least 55%) of the local community supports. Green Trust delivers wind and solar projects that work for the local community through: community profit; community ownership; affordable green electricity supply for local households and businesses; lease income for landowners that is competitive with commercial developers. Green Trust's community interest company (CIC) legal structure and objectives mean the profit made by each project must go to the local community. Contact Jake Burnyeat, Managing Director, for more information.

Web: http://www.greentrustwind.co.uk
Email: jakeburnyeat@greentrustwind.co.uk
Phone: 07815 014 540
Address: Falmouth Ambulance Building, Quarry Hill,
Falmouth, Cornwall TR11 2BP

WAVE HUB

The Wave Hub allows developers of wave energy devices to test new wave energy technology. It is a grid-connected offshore facility near Hayle for the large scale testing of technologies that generate electricity from the power of the waves. It leases space to wave energy device developers and exists to support the development of marine renewable energy around the world.

Web: http://www.wavehub.co.uk

Email: enquiries@wavehub.co.uk

Phone: 01736 800 290

Address: John Harvey House, 24 Foundry Square, Hayle TR27 4HH

WEST CORNWALL COMMUNITY RENEWABLES

WCCR is a new social enterprise that aims to develop local community owned assets (particularly those that generate renewable energy) and so support  the community move towards becoming self-sufficient in renewable energy. Its social business model will put ownership in the hands of the community rather than private investors and thus serve broader local interests.

Email: info@wc-cr.co.uk

Address: care of 1 Tregeseal Row, St Just, Penzance TR19 7PJ

THE CO-OPERATIVE ENERGY

The Co-operative is a wide-ranging business owned by its customers. It has only entered the energy market in 2011 having looked at energy for some time, believing that the public have been poorly served. The Co-operative's members guide them on how the organisation should behave as an ethical business, a responsible citizen and a committed campaigner. They support renewable energy and are planning to ensure that, by April 2012, the carbon content of their electricity is less than half the national average. They avoid coal but they do support nuclear power, thinking that a multi-pronged approach is needed if the UK is to meet its climate change targets in the medium term.

Web: http://www.cooperativeenergy.coop

Email: info@cooperativeenergy.coop

Phone: 0800 954 0693

Address: Warwick Technology Pk, Gallows Hill, Warwick CV34 6DA

EBICO

Ebico's strongest feature is that
it's the only not-for-profit energy
supplier in the UK. Renewable
energy production is not a core

part of their offering but they have an interesting tariff called
Equiclimate. It is a carbon offsetting service for customers who want
to redress the effects on the environment of their own energy use.

Web: **http://www.ebico.org.uk**

Email: **info@ebico.org.uk**

Phone: **0800 458 7689**

Address: **Ebico Ltd, PO Box 354, Witney, Oxfordshire OX29 7WN**

ECOTRICITY

All the green electricity in Ecotricity's
"New Energy" tariff comes from
their own windmills but is topped
up with 'brown' electricity which

they buy from the wholesale market. Customers on the "New Energy
Plus" tariff have their top-up from another producer's green electricity
making it a 100% renewable supply. Ecotricity's main selling point is
that - by percentage of turnover - they are the biggest investor in new
renewable productive capacity within the UK.

Web: **http://www.ecotricity.co.uk**

Email: **home@ecotricity.co.uk**

Phone: **01453 756 111**

Address: **Unicorn House, Russell Street, Stroud GL5 3AX**

GOOD ENERGY

Good Energy is the UK's only
100% renewable electricity supplier.
That means that they guarantee
to supply exactly the amount of
electricity that their customers

consume either from their own renewable energy production or
else from bought-in renewable energy supplies. Of all the electricity
suppliers they are probably the keenest on customers reducing their

demand and very much encourage micro-generation. 'Green gas' (or biomethane) is still some years away from being economically viable, so Good Energy have developed a product to work in conjunction with their gas tariff which will encourage the growth of renewable heat generation in the UK.

Web: http://www.goodenergy.co.uk
Email: enquiries@goodenergy.co.uk
Phone: 0845 456 1640
Address: **Monkton Reach, Monkton Hill, Chippenham, Wiltshire SN15 1EE**

COMMUNITY ENERGY PLUS

Community Energy Plus is an award-winning social enterprise that provides complete energy answers to help householders in Cornwall enjoy warmer, energy efficient homes as part of a more  sustainable future. Since 1997 they have worked in partnership with a wide range of public, private and third sector organisations to support a variety of innovative projects relating to energy efficiency and renewable energy including community ownership models. For local and free independent advice on energy efficiency to help you save money and enjoy a warmer, healthier home, as well as access to grants for insulation and heating and information on renewable technologies, visit their website or call the Freephone advice line in Cornwall on 0800 954 1956.

Web: http://www.cep.org.uk
Email: enquiries@cep.org.uk
Phone: 01209 614 975
Address: **3-4 East Pool, Tolvaddon Energy Park, Camborne, Cornwall TR14 0HX**

OPEN BRIEFING

Open Briefing is the world's first civil society intelligence agency; an accessible platform for insight and analysis on key energy, defence,  security and foreign policy issues. They provide open source intelligence assessments and independent security briefings, so that a better informed civil society can properly engage with peace and security debates. Resource Security and Climate Change are a major area of interest for Open Briefing. And it all comes out of Penwith!

Web: **http://www.openbriefing.org**

RENEWABLE ENERGY OFFICE FOR CORNWALL

The REOC vision for Cornwall is: "To become an internationally recognised centre of excellence for a wide range of renewable energy technologies and to develop these so as to meet a high proportion of the county's energy needs." It aims to develop a cluster of renewable energy technologies. It will help co-ordinate development, provide information on possible sources of funding and lobby, when necessary.  REOC also provides emerging renewable energy companies with a useful forum for exchange of information and the potential for joint partnerships where two or more different technologies might produce a better business solution than one - for example wave and tidal stream working together, or anaerobic digestion sharing a hook up to the grid with an onshore wind farm and energy crop gasification plant. REOC feels that Cornwall could not only become more self sufficient in energy than any other region in the UK and EU but it could also, as the most visited rural county in the UK, provide a renewable energy showcase for others to learn from and emulate.

Web: **http://www.reoc.info**
Email: **contact@reoc.info**
Phone: **01326 572 720**
Address: **Monument House, 58 Coinagehall St, Helston TR13 8EL**

YOUGEN

Helps you find and compare renewable energy installers, suppliers and information. They can make it easy for you to improve  the energy efficiency of your home and buy with confidence. Use their site to: Find out the truth about renewable energy from an independent source; read tips from their energy experts; ask a question and learn from other people's comments; help others by sharing your experience of renewable energy or recommending your supplier; and find people who have already installed the technology you're interested in or find a local supplier to install it for you. Phone line: Mon to Fri, 9am to 5pm.

Web: **http://www.yougen.co.uk**
Phone: **0845 450 9418**
Address: **Meadway, Cotford, Sidmouth, Devon EX10 0SH**

UNIVERSITY OF EXETER - RENEWABLE ENERGY

Undergraduate course leads to professionally accredited vocational training with extensive field work and an industrial placement.
Postgraduate research opportunities enhanced by expert academic supervision and excellent field and laboratory research facilities. Their research expertise spans energy policy, marine renewables, bio-fuels, electrical power and networks, wind, photo-voltaic and thermal technologies. Their academics are committed to working with a diverse range of stakeholders to ensure a better informed and more inclusive approach to sustainable energy solutions.

Web: **http://emps.exeter.ac.uk/renewable-energy**
Address: **Camborne School of Mines**
College of Engineering, Mathematics and Physical Sciences, University of Exeter Cornwall Campus, Penryn TR10 9EZ

Energy

Food and Agriculture

In many ways modern farming has become a process of turning oil into food! The soil is so damaged that it does little other than hold the plant up. Farmers have to add chemical fertilisers to each new crop to maintain growth and the monoculture system necessitates the ongoing use of pesticides and herbicides. All these products are oil based and if we take into account the fuel that is needed for farm machinery, food processing and transportation we can see how the industry is completely dependent upon on fossil fuels. It may not be surprising either to find that the carbon footprint of the food sector is higher than that of trains, planes and vehicles combined. The global food system is only enabled by plentiful oil and is truly "efficient" in one area only: reducing the cost of food at the till. But "cheaper" food has hidden costs – both social and environmental. These include water pollution and food chain contamination by agro-chemicals, mass deforestation and biodiversity loss, fisheries depletion, soil erosion and destruction of rural communities through intensive farming and production of greenhouse gases. Much of the food we buy comes from outside of Cornwall (outside the UK even) and the system is vulnerable to transport strikes, global price structures and ultimately, of course, oil shortages. Dramatic oil price rises could create a crisis situation in which we could see major food shortages. It is vitally important that we build some resilience and reliability into our food systems. A lot of great things are happening in Penwith already but we need to work closely with the farming and business community to further re-localise food growing and distribution infrastructure as well as encouraging individual and community action to grow more of our own food.

ALLOTMENTS

Hayle
- Hayle Town Council
  01736 755005
  townclerk@hayletowncouncil.net
- Hayle Allotment Society
  http://hayleallotments.org.uk

Ludgvan
- Ludgvan Parish Council
  01736 751790, edwr393@aol.com

Penzance
- Penzance Town Council (sites at Lescudjack, Leskinnick, Crankan, Trannack, Gulval, Love Lane, Alverton, Mennaye, Penlee Point)
  01736 363405, info@penzancetowncouncil.co.uk
- Cornwall Council (site at Madron)
  estatesmanagement@cornwall.gov.uk

St Ives
- St Ives Town Council
  01736 797840, stivestowncouncil@gmail.com

St Just
- Some allotments in use already, more on the way.
  info@bosaverncommunityfarm.org.uk

United Kingdom
- National Society of Allaotment & Leisure Gardeners
  http://www.nsalg.org.uk
  01536 266576, natsoc@nsalg.org.uk

BOSAVERN COMMUNITY FARM

A Cornwall Council owned organic farm on the outskirts of St Just which has been used to encourage new farmers into agriculture since WWI. Proposals from the local community led to a short lease being granted  to the Lands End Peninsula Community Land Trust. This is to show that the community can manage the farm and to raise the funds to purchase the site. They are growing vegetables, keeping chickens, pigs, and turkeys. It is envisaged that farm purchase will be facilitated by a community share issue and other funding possibilities.

Food and Agriculture

Web: http://www.bosaverncommunityfarm.org.uk

Email: info@bosaverncommunityfarm.org.uk

Phone: 01736 788 454

Address: Bosavern Community Farm, St Just, Penzance TR19 7RD

BREWING AND WINEMAKING

Hayle

- Paradise Brewery
Paradise Park, Trelissick Road,
Hayle TR27 4HY. 01736 753974

Newlyn

- Cornish Mead Company
http://www.cornishmead.co.uk
The Mead House, Newlyn, Penzance TR18 5QF. 01736 363942

Penzance

- Polgoon Vineyard
http://www.polgoon.co.uk
Rosehill, Penzance TR20 8TE. 01736 333946, kim@polgoon.co.uk

Sancreed

- Tregonibris Fine Wines
http://www.tregonebriswines.co.uk
Tregonebris Farmhouse, Sancreed, Penzance TR20 8RQ
01736 810465, info@tregonebriswines.co.uk

CAFÉS

Hayle

- Johnny's Café
http://www.johnnyscafe.co.uk
50-51 Penpol Trc, Hayle TR27 4BQ
01736 755 928, hello@johnnyscafe.co.uk

Penzance

- Archie Browns
http://www.archiebrowns.co.uk
Bread Street, Penzance, Cornwall TR18 2EQ
01736 362 828, hello@archiebrowns.co.uk
- The Honey Pot
5 The Parade, Penzance TR18 4BU
01736 368686, kath.e.hawkins@fsmail.net

Food and
Agriculture

- Manna's Diner
  Unit 23, Wharfside Shopping Centre, Penzance TR18 2GB
  01736 350604
- Waves Café Bar
  29 Causewayhead, Penzance TR18 2SP
  01736 600014, taylor_darren1@sky.com

Perranuthnoe

- Peppercorn Kitchen Café
  http://www.peppercornkitchen.co.uk
  Lynfield Yard, Perranuthnoe, Penzance TR20 9NE
  01736 719584, contact@peppercornkitchen.co.uk

Sennen

- Apple Tree Café
  http://www.theappletreecafe.co.uk
  Trevescan, Sennen, Penzance, Cornwall TR19 7RD
  07990 500082, theappletreecafe@ymail.com

St Just

- The Cook Book
  http://www.thecookbookstjust.co.uk
  4 Cape Cornwall Street, St Just, Penzance, Cornwall TR19 7JZ
  01736 787266, info@thecookbookstjust.co.uk

CONFECTIONERY

Newlyn

- Rweena Baldwin Chocolates
  31 New Road, Newlyn,
  Penzance TR18 5PZ
  01736 360548, rweenabaldwin@hotmail.com

Sancreed

- Sweet Moments
  7 Beacon Estate, Sancreed, Penzance TR20 8QR
  01736 81106, siggihawken@gmail.com

St Ives

- The Enormous Little Bakery
  http://www.theelb.co.uk
  01736 795945, mica@theelb.co.uk
- Adore Macarons
  http://www.adoremacarons.com
  3 Penbeagle Vean, St Ives TR26 2EN
  01736 799575, monika@peterburgess.net

Food and Agriculture

THE CO-OPERATIVE FOOD

If you must use a supermarket then the least worst one that you can use has to be The Co-operative Food. As part of the largest consumer co-op in the world it's owned by its members. It doesn't cost anything to join and if you have your card swiped every time that you purchase something then you'll receive your share of the "dividend". As a small player in the market The Co-operative is unlikely to be as cheap as the really big supermarkets but it's surprising how much comes back in the form of the dividend and other member benefits. Most importantly you know where the money you spend there is going and – as a member – you have the opportunity to vote for people to go on the committees which control the organisation. The Co-operative is well represented in Penwith.

Hayle
- 18 Copper Terrace, Hayle TR27 4EB

Penzance
- 114-117 Market Jew Street, Penzance TR18 2LD
- 6 Queens Square, Penzance TR18 2JJ
- The Promenade, Wherrytown, Penzance TR18 4NP

Newlyn
- 18 The Strand, Newlyn, Penzance TR18 5HN

St Ives
- The Stennack, St Ives TR26 1DB
- Royal Square, St Ives TR26 2ND
- 13-14 Tregenna Place, St Ives TR26 1SD

St Just
- Corner House, St Just, Penzance TR19 7HE

Web: **http://www.co-operative.coop**

DAIRY

Heamoor
- Davas Yogurt
  Bone Farm, Heamoor,
  Penzance, Cornwall TR20 8UJ
  01736 368 708, davasyogurt@msn.com

Food and Agriculture

Penzance
- Mounts Bay Dairy
  Units 6/7/8 Rospeath Lane, Penzance TR20 8DU
  01736 741216, mountsbaydairy@gmail.com

Zennor
- Moomaid of Zennor Ice Cream
  http://www.moomaidofzennor.com
  Tremedda Farm, Zennor, St Ives TR26 3BS
  01736 799603, info@moomaidofzennor.com

FOREST GARDENING AT CORNWALL

Agroforestry Services have their own Forest Garden and practise Forest Gardening and Agroforestry

Forest Gardening at Cornwall

techniques suitable for a temperate climate. Forest Gardening and Agroforestry is the interaction of plants that are edible, medicinal, or of some use to mankind and the eco system alike. It integrates aspects of forestry, agriculture and horticulture, but focuses primarily on perennials, trees, shrubs, herbaceous, ground cover and climbing plants. The interaction between plants and the eco system is a multidimensional one. They offer landscaping, plant supplies, consultancy as well as garden tours, talks and courses.

Web: **http://www.forestgardeningatcornwall.co.uk**

Phone: **01326 250 090**

Address: **Penjerrick Hill, Budock Water, Falmouth TR11 5ED**

THE GARDEN LADY

Vicki Marshall is a gardener, plantswoman and nursery owner based on the southern slopes of Godolphin Hill. In addition to roses, the nursery also produces a wide range of herbs and a selection of interesting, often aromatic plants for the garden. The Garden Lady is to be found at many Farmers Markets and local produce markets in the area.

Web: **http://thegardenlady.co.uk**

Email: **vicki@thegardenlady.co.uk**

Phone: **01736 762 124**

Address: **2 Trewithen Terrace, Godolphin, Helston TR13 9TQ**

GROWERS

Gulval

- Incredible Crops  **GROWERS**
  Trezelah Barn. Trezelah, Gulval,
  Penzance TR20 8XD
  01736 333773, john.samuels@virgin.net
- Kenegie Organics
  Kenegie Home Farm, Gulval, Penzance TR20 8YN
  01736 333457, joffrorke@tiscali.co.uk

Hayle

- Heather Lane Nursery
  Hayle TR27 6NF
  01736 740198

Lamorna

- Lamorna Fayre
  1 The Nook, Penberth Valley, St Buryan,
  Penzance, Cornwall TR19 6HJ
  01736 811285, corin@acorin.orangehome.co.uk

Ludgvan

- Food for the Future
  Fields at Castle Gate, Ludgvan,
  Penzance, Cornwall TR20 8BG
  07973 813607, dax.ansell@realideas.org
- Lowarth Brough
  http://www.lowarthbrogh.blogspot.com
  Lower Tremenheere Farm, Ludgvan, Penzance TR20 8XG
  01736 333 927, lowarthbrogh@gmail.com

Morvah

- Keigwin Natural Growers
  Keigwin Farmhouse, Keigwin, Morvah, Penzance TR19 7TS
  01736 786425, gilly@yewtreegallery.com

MEAT

Crowlas

- Rospeath Farm Organics
  http://www.rospeathfarm.co.uk **MEAT**
  Rospeath Farm, Crowlas,
  Penzance, Cornwall TR20 9BL
  01736 740286, paul@rospeathfarm.co.uk

Morvah
- Trevean Farm
  http://www.ntwestcornwall.co.uk/category/trevean-farm
  Trevowhan, Morvah, Penzance TR20 8YU
  01736 787234, guy.clegg@nationaltrust.org.uk

Newbridge
- Higher Bostraze Farm   http://www.higherbostrazefarm.com
  Newbridge, Penzance TR20 8PT
  07754 992889, della@higherbostrazefarm.com

Sancreed
- Ewephoric Lamb
  http://www.ewephoricryelands.com
  An Chapel Coth, Trevarthan, Grumbla, Sancreed,
  Penzance TR20 8QY
  01736 786173, pandj@coth.wanadoo.co.uk

St Ives
- St Ives Beef
  Little Trevalgan, Trevalgan Farm, St Ives TR26 3BJ
  01736 796529, info@stivesbeef.co.uk

St Levan
- Chegwidden Farm
  St Levan, Penzance TR19 6LP
  01736 810516, halls@chegwiddenfarm.com

St Just
- Vivian Olds Ltd   http://www.vivianolds.co.uk
  2 Chapel Street, St Just, Penzance, Cornwall TR19 7HS
  01736 788520, mail@vivianolds.co.uk

MILLING AND BAKING

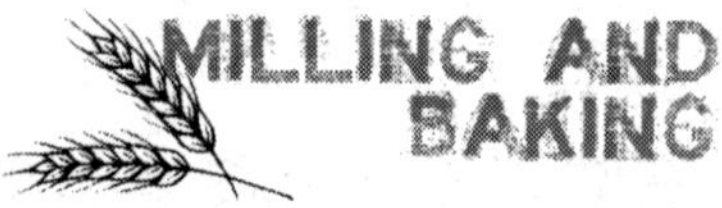

Goldsithney
- Cornish Fruitcake Company
  www.cornishfruitcakecompany.co.uk
- Gears Farm, Gears Lane,
  Goldsithney, Penzance TR20 9LB
  01736 710030, gilly@cornishfruitcakecompany.co.uk

Helston
- Hope's Bread
  http://www.hopesbread.co.uk
  Tregarne Farm, Manaccan, Helston, Cornwall TR12 6EW
  01326 281097, hopeoneill@hotmail.com

Lelant Downs
- Boojum
  Count House, Trencrom, Lelant Downs,
  Hayle, Cornwall TR27 6NU
  01736 740038, lorraineharvey@gmail.com

Marazion
- The Occasional Tart   http://www.theoccasionaltart.com
  c/o The Barn, Gwallon Lane, Marazion,
  Penzance, Cornwall TR17 0HW
  07890 325899, theoccasionaltart@yahoo.co.uk

Nancledra
- Ruby June's Indian Kitchen   http://www.junesindiankitchen.co.uk
  Melyngy, Nancledra, Penzance, Cornwall TR20 8NB
  01736 741482, june@junesindiankitchen.co.uk

St Erth
- Jim's Bakery
  18 Fore Street, St Erth, Hayle, Cornwall TR27 6HT
  01736 756720, sally.navin@btinternet.com

Zennor
- Trewey Mill
  Wayside Museum and Trewey Mill, Zennor,
  St Ives, Cornwall TR26 3DA
  01736 796946, sarapriddle@btinternet.com

PEAT PROJECT

The PEAT Project Is an open
gardening programme which
includes a wide range of informal
learning activities aimed at helping
people gain valuable skills, and
acquiring accredited qualifications

whilst promoting a healthier lifestyle. They have an acre of prime
growing land on the outskirts of Penzance where they are teaching
the basics of growing vegetables. People benefit through raised
self confidence and self esteem, gaining new skills, enhanced
employability plus improved health and wellbeing.

   Web: http://www.peatproject.org
   Email: val@pcdt.org.uk
   Phone: 07595 567676

PENWITH & HELSTON ORGANIC GARDENERS AND GROWERS

POGG is the Penwith part of this organisation. Both groups are affiliated to Garden Organic, the national organic association, and they have the same aims: to help their members gain from each other's experiences of gardening and growing using organic methods by pooling ideas and knowledge. They also aim to promote the organic movement to a wider audience, as well as among manufacturers and retailers. POGG and HOGG work closely, with the structure of both groups kept to the minimum. They hold friendly informal meetings which are an opportunity for exchanging tips, contacts and information. Summer meetings take the form of visits to gardens (members' and others); speakers and topics of interest are arranged for the winter.

Web: http://www.phogg.org.uk

Email: p-hogg@hotmail.com

PENWITH ENVIRONMENTAL NETWORK

Penwith Environmental Network was set up in 1984 and became a charity in 1987. For many years it ran an open centre for the public to access information about environmental issues in Penwith. The charity has gradually evolved into a network promoting environmental issues in a local context. Increasing environmental awareness through education and networking with other groups in Penwith. The main body of its work is now centred on the Edible Forest, wildlife meadow and community garden at Love Lane, Badger's Garden Community Supported Agriculture scheme and managing Millennium Woods. It has been awarded a grant to create Penwith Edible Forest; a mixture of fruit trees and shrubs planted to mimic forest layers with the aim to maximise fruit yield, be low maintenance and have maximum wildlife value. PEN now hosts practical courses in all aspects of forest gardening.

Web: http://www.p-e-n.org.uk

Email: info@p-e-n.org.uk

Address: c/o Penwith Centre, Parade Street, Penzance TR18 4BX

Food and Agriculture

PENZANCE FOOD BANK

Churches Together in the Penzance Area recognised that increasing numbers of people in the town were truly starting to get stressed by **Penzance Food Bank** failing "to make ends meet." So in 2011 a team of volunteers came together to create the Food Bank. A number of local supermarkets allow for a Food Bank collection box to be situated around the exit tills; and churches at the back of the church. These collection boxes, having been filled by members of the general public, are then emptied twice a week by volunteers. Recipients are identified through a voucher system organised by Social Services, CAB, Schools, Doctors and Health visitors, PHA, Job Centre Plus, YMCA, Community Police, and other caring agencies. A Food Bank has recently started in Hayle as well.

Web: http://www.churchestogetherinpenzance.co.uk

PRESERVES

Penzance

- Sisleys Cornish Preserves
  www.sisleyscornishpreserves.com
  Pendennis Road, Penzance,
  Cornwall TR18 2BE
  01736 332464, info@sisleyscornishpreserves.com

Sennen
- Sara's Chilli Relish
  Peace and Plenty, Gwyner, Sennen,
  Penzance, Cornwall TR19 6LP
  sara@stantonnadin.wanadoo.co.uk

RESTAURANTS

Halsetown

- The Halsetown Inn
  http://www.halsetowninn.co.uk
  Halsetown, St Ives
  Cornwall TR26 3NA
  01736 795583, info@halsetowninn.co.uk

Food and Agriculture

Mousehole

- The Cornish Range   http://www.cornishrange.co.uk
  6 Chapel Street, Mousehole, Penzance TR19 6SB
  01736 731488, enquiries@cornishrange.co.uk
- The Old Coastguard
  http://www.oldcoastguardhotel.co.uk
  The Parade, Mousehole, Penzance, Cornwall TR19 6PR
  01736 731222, enquiries@oldcoastguardhotel.co.uk

Penzance

- Archie Browns   http://www.archiebrowns.co.uk
  Bread Street, Penzance TR18 2EQ
  01736 362828, hello@archiebrowns.co.uk
- The Bakehouse Restaurant
  http://www.bakehouserestaurant.co.uk
  Old Bakehouse Lane, Chapel Street, Penzance TR18 4AE
  01736 331331, info@bakehouserestaurant.co.uk
- The Bay Restaurant
  http://www.baypenzance.co.uk
  Britons Hill, Penzance TR18 3AE
  01736 366890, eat@thebaypenzance.co.uk
- The Boatshed Cafe Bar Restaurant
  http://www.boatshed.org.uk
  Wharf Road, Penzance TR18 4AS
  01736 366746, nigel.waller@bosuns.org
- Untitled by Robert Wright
  http://www.untitledbyrobertwright.com
  Abbey Street, Penzance TR18 4AR
  01736 448022, enquiries@untitledbyrobertwright.com

St Ives

- Alfresco   http://www.alfrescocafebar.co.uk
  The Wharf, St Ives TR26 1LG
  01736 793737, joy@alfrescocafebar.co.uk
- Blas Burgerworks   http://www.blasburgerworks.co.uk
  The Warren, St Ives, Cornwall TR26 2EA
  01736 797272, info@blasburgerworks.co.uk
- Queens Hotel   http://www.queenshotelstives.com
  High Street, St Ives, Cornwall TR26 1RR
  01736 796468, info@queenshotelstives.com
- Spinachio's   http://www.spinacios.co.uk
  Old Custom House, Wharf Road, St Ives, Cornwall TR26 1LF
  01736 798818, info@spinacios.co.uk

St Just
- Commercial Hotel
  http://www.commercial-hotel.co.uk
  13 Market Square, St Just, Penzance TR19 7HE
  01736 788455, enquiries@commercial-hotel.co.uk
- Kings Arms
  http://www.wix.com/neillmaguire/kings-arms-st
  5 Market Square, St Just, Penzance TR19 7HF
  01736 788545, kingsatstjust@yahoo.co.uk

Treen
- The Gurnard's Head
  http://www.gurnardshead.co.uk
  Treen, St Ives TR26 3DE
  01736 796928 - enquiries@gurnardshead.co.uk

SEAFOOD

Hayle
- Hayle Mackerel Liners Ass.
  www.linecaughtmackerel.org.uk
  Tasty Mac Pac Ltd., Unit 1,
  Marsh Lane Ind Est, Hayle TR27 5JR
  01736 796506, info@linecaughtmackerel.org.uk

SEAFOOD

Sennen
- Crabby Jacks
  Hesva, Mayon Sennen, Penzance TR19 7AD
  01736 871297, crabbyjackspz6@aol.com

SELLERS

- Wholefood.net
  www.wholefood.net
  PO Box 147, Penzance TR19 6WD
  01736 810015

 SELLERS

- Healthy Boxes
  http://healthyboxes.co.uk
  07966 897561, louise.reynolds@hotmail.co.uk

Newlyn
- J H Turner & Co
  The Coombe, Newlyn, Penzance, Cornwall TR18 5HS
  http://www.jhturner.co.uk
  01736 363726, robin@turnerjh.force9.co.uk

Food and Agriculture

- Newlyn Cheese and Charcuterie
  http://www.newlyncheese.co.uk
  1 New Road, Newlyn, Penzance,
  Cornwall TR18 5PZ
  01736 368714, info@newlyncheese.co.uk

Penzance

- Archie Browns
  http://www.archiebrowns.co.uk
  Bread Street, Penzance TR18 2EQ
  01736 362828, hello@archiebrowns.co.uk
- The Cornish Hen Deli
  27a Market Place, Penzance TR18 2JD
  01736 350223, sarah@thecornishhen.plus.com
- The Granary
  15D Causewayhead, Penzance,
  Cornwall TR18 2SN
  01736 361869

St Just

- Stones
  2 Market Square, St Just, Penzance, Cornwall TR19 7HF
  07891 547297, claire@justfineart.eclipse.co.uk

St Levan

- Treen Local Produce Shop
  Treen, St Levan, Penzance TR19 6LF
  01736 811285, corin@acorin.orangehome.co.uk

TREVASKIS FARM

Trevaskis Farm offers just about
everything. You can pick your own fruit
and vegetables, buy produce from
their farm shop, eat at their restaurant
and learn about organic farming.

They also offer opportunities for schools, colleges, adult education and
social groups to learn more about the origins of the food they eat.

Web: **http://www.trevaskisfarm.co.uk**
Email: **hello@trevaskisfarm.co.uk**
Phone: **01209 714 009**
Address: **Gwinear, Hayle, Cornwall TR27 5JQ**

Food and Agriculture

WEST CORNWALL FARMERS' MARKETS

This is an innovative scheme directly targeting support to farming families. It's been set up to increase micro producers' ability to sell food directly to local people, thereby reducing food miles and packaging while supporting the rural economy.

Web: http://www.wcfm.org.uk

Paul
* Paul Farmers' Market. Every Wednesday, 10.00 - 12.00.
  The Village Hall, Paul, Penzance TR19 6UG. 07866 75827

Pendeen
* Pendeen Farmers' Market. First and Third Saturday of every month, 10.00 – 13.00. The Centre of Pendeen, Pendeen, Penzance TR19 7SE.
  07706 659784, yvonnebristow@blue-earth.co.uk

Penzance
* Penzance Country Market. Every Thursday 08.30 - 12.30.
  St John's Hall, Alverton Street, Penzance TR18 2QR.
  07807 448 374, penzancecountrymarket@gmail.com
* Penzance Farmers' Market. Every Friday, 09.00 - 14.00.
  St John's Hall, Alverton St, Penzance TR18 2QR. 07809 503610

Sennen
* Sennen Farmers' Market. Every Tuesday, 09.00 - 12.00.
  Sennen Community Centre, Mayon Green, Sennen TR19 7AW.
  01736 871491, contact@samphirefoodevents.co.uk

St Buryan
* St Buryan Farmers' Market. Second and Fourth Saturday of every month, 09.30 - 12.30. St Buryan Village Hall, St Buryan, Penzance, TR19 6ES. 01736 810349

St Erth
* St Erth Farmers' Market. Every Saturday, 10.00 - 12.00.
  Methodist Chapel, St Erth, Hayle TR27 6HL.
  01736 757030, alex.sheff@xalt.co.uk

St Ives
* St Ives Farmers' Market. Every Thursday, 09.30 - 14.00.
  The Guildhall, Street-an-Pol, St Ives TR26 2DS.
  01736 795387, info@stivesfarmersmarket.co.uk

Food and Agriculture

WEST CORNWALL FOOD

This website will help you in your quest to buy and eat local food. You know that you have bought locally when you can find out who  produced your food. Local food will also be seasonal food. We may be able to buy almost any food at any time of the year but the cost of this has been great: vegetables are picked before they are ripe; varieties are chosen for long shelf life and transportation instead of taste; and food is overpackaged and treated.

Web: http://www.westcornwallfood.org.uk

W W O O F

WWOOF stands for World Wide Opportunities on Organic Farms and WWOOF UK holds a list of organic farms, gardens and smallholdings, all offering food and accommodation in exchange for practical help on their land. Hosts do not expect you to know a lot about farming when you arrive, but they do expect you to be willing to learn and able to fit in with their lifestyle. The list of hosts is available by joining WWOOF UK for a membership fee. Once you have the list, it is up to you to contact hosts directly to arrange your stay. Volunteers do not pay to stay with hosts and hosts do not pay volunteers for their help. There are several local WWOOF hosts.

WWOOF UK
World Wide Opportunities on Organic Farms

Web: http://www.wwoof.org.uk
Address: PO Box 2154, Winslow, Buckingham MK18 3WS

WILD FOOD

- Fat Hen
  http://www.fathen.org
  Gwenmenhir, Boscawen-noon
  Farm, St Buryan, Penzance,
  Cornwall TR19 6EH
  01736 810156
- Rachel Lambert - Wild Walks
  http://www.wildwalks-southwest.co.uk
  07903 412014, rachel@wildwalks-southwest.co.uk

Health and Wellbeing

In many ways the idea of preventative medicine – which many of us practice – is exactly like the Transition model ... making changes now so that we avoid hardships later on when changes might not be so easy to make. So by maintaining a level of good health we aim to prevent something worse happening later on – keeping a good body weight to protect against Type 2 Diabetes or giving up smoking to prevent heart disease for example. It's important to distinguish between health on the one hand, and the health care system. The health systems of developed countries, including our own, are heavily dependent on fossil fuels, for example; our large hospitals are very resource intensive, one in twenty journeys on our roads is associated with health care and many of the drugs and medical consumables are derived from oil. However, it is possible to maintain good health in a population with relatively few resources, for example, the life expectancy in Cuba is higher than that in the USA, which spends many times more on its health care system. This is because health care delivered locally, and promptly, is more effective at keeping people healthy. In addition, because oil is scarce, the Cubans walk and cycle more, and generally lead a more active life than their American neighbours. Decentralising services wherever possible and prioritising local sourcing of food and materials is an important priority for sustainable health in Penwith. We also need to develop healthy living programmes in partnership with others, implement reskilling and retraining projects and develop green herbal medicines as possible alternatives to pharmaceuticals. Health education, including nutrition, bodywork and movement and positive thinking will all be key for a smooth transition.

Health and Wellbeing

BRITISH RED CROSS

They offer a range of first aid courses covering various life saving skills that are suitable for everyone. Courses range from 2 to

7 hours. You don't need to have any previous first aid knowledge or experience as their public courses include lots of practical exercises to give you confidence in dealing with a real life emergency.

Web: http://www.redcrossfirstaidtraining.co.uk
Address: Red Cross Hse, Lighterage Hill, Newham, Truro TR1 2XR

CATCH A WAVE - BIG BEACH EXPERIENCE

Watersports social enterprise based in south west Cornwall aims to use watersports as a means of improving health and wellbeing, especially of the disadvantaged. Fully qualified surf instructors and complementary therapists. Also

free beachwalks for health and wellbeing across Penwith plus many beach cleans in association with Keep Britain Tidy.

Web: http://www.catchawaveuk.com
Email: info@catchawaveuk
Phone: 07778 598 955
Address: c/o Penwith Centre, Parade Street, Penzance TR18 4BU

CORNWALL HEALTHY LIVING CENTRE

CHLC aims to provide a vehicle for health professionals, voluntary and community sector organisations and individuals to work together to improve health and well-being

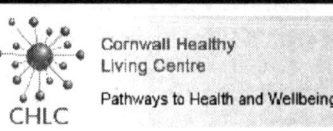

and reduce health inequality. They provide a proactive and holistic approach to tackling underlying health problems by linking people through the following schemes: GP Recommendation Scheme; Central Information and Support Scheme; Volunteer Recruitment Scheme; Well-being Activities.

Web: http://wchlc.org.uk

CORNWALL RAMBLERS

The Penwith and Kerrier group of Cornwall Ramblers covers the west of Cornwall from Portreath on the north-west coast, west to Land's End, easterly along the south coast, around the Lizard peninsula and up to and including the Helford river estuary.

The landscape is varied with the coast path, beaches, harbours, archaeological sites, old mining sites, open moors and hidden valleys. They have a walk at least once a week all year round led by local leaders.

Web: **http://www.cornwallramblers.org.uk**

Email: **sylvronan@btinternet.com**

Phone: **01736 740 542**

Address: **c/o Trebant, Ludgvan Churchtown, Penzance TR20 8HH**

CTC CORNWALL

CTC Cornwall is a "Local Group" of the Cyclists' Touring Club. A Local Group represents CTC members in a particular geographical area. In the case

of CTC Cornwall this is the whole of Cornwall. Thus if you are a CTC Member living in Cornwall, you are automatically a member of CTC Cornwall. CTC Cornwall is in its infancy - the group was formed in March 2008. There is usually a ride from Penzance on a Sunday.

Web: **http://ctccornwall.org.uk**

Email: **info@ctccornwall.org.uk**

CYCLING

Penzance

- Penwith Midweek Cycle Group Ride every Thursday morning from Penzance, usually meeting at St John's Hall.
  David Harvey, 01736 365019

DANCE

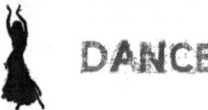

Hayle
- Hayle Line Dancing Club,
  Mon evenings at Hayle Methodist
  Church. 01736 752610

Marazion
- Tango
  http://www.tangogowild.com
  Beginners lessons in Marazion and Camborne. 078772 022751

Newlyn
- Circle Dance Mona
  Community dances from around the world at the Newlyn Centre.
  Thursday evenings and alternate Tuesday mornings.
  01736 361010
- Shiva Shakti Dance Suzannah Uren
  Healing dance class for women on Wednesday evenings at the
  Newlyn Centre. 07536 005857

Pendeen
- Dance Into Fitness
  Classes for the over 50s on Tuesday mornings at Pendeen
  Womens Institute Hall.
  Caroline Shanche, 07773 669667

Penzance
- The Big Dance Company
  http://www.thebigdancecompany.co.uk Many different classes
  suitable from age 3 to adult. Main studio in Penzance.
- Salsa @ the Source
  West Penwith Salsa on Wednesday 8.00 to10.45pm at the Source
  in Penzance. Classes for beginners and the more experienced.
  01736 363236 or 711524
- Hotstep Salsa
  http://www.hotstepsalsa.co.uk
  Sundays at the Lugger Hotel in Penzance. Chris, 01209 611807
  or 07970 397736, chris@hotstepsalsa.co.uk
- Eastern Dance
  Monday evenings at Penzance YMCA
  Liz Newman, 01326 564744, newlizwiz@btinternet.com,
- Zumba Claire
  Tuesday and Thursday evenings at Penzance YMCA.
  07859 242735

St Erth
- Hotstep Salsa
http://www.hotstepsalsa.co.uk Fridays in St Erth Village Hall.
Chris, 01209 611807 or 07970 397736, chris@hotstepsalsa.co.uk

St Ives
- Belly dance
http://www.bellydancestives.co.uk Friday evenings at St Ives
Operatics Club. Helena, 07941 242973

St Just
- Salsa
Monday evenings at the Royal British Legion in St Just.
martinwebster1959@gmail.com
- Dance Into Fitness
Classes for the over 50s on Fridays in St Just.
Caroline Shanche 07773 669667

FELDENKRAIS

Penzance, St Ives
- Shelagh O'Neill PhD MFG(UK), **FELDENKRAIS**
http://www.nicefeldenkrais.co.uk
Offers classes and workshops in
awareness through movement and gives one-to-one functional
integration sessions. Wed am: St Ives; Fri am: Penzance.
21 Morrab Place, Penzance TR18 4DQ
01736 365783, shelagh.oneill@feldenkrais.co.uk

KEEP FIT

Newlyn
- RS Fitness Newlyn
A gentle exercise class for people
with varying health conditions
and low fitness. 01736 369460

Penzance
- Cardiac Rehab
Friday mornings at Penzance YMCA, mainly 50+
Chris Smith, 01736 351 479, glendeep@tiscali.co.uk
- Gwellhean fitness
Circuit training with a personal plan on tuesday afternoons at
Penzance YMCA. Shane, 01209 21825 or 07866 687085

- Fitness and Circuit Training Boot Camp
  Karen and Bill, 01736 787856
- Penzance Leisure Centre
  http://www.leisurecentre.com
  St Clare, Penzance TR18 3QW.
  Runs a full fitness timetable Booking required. 01736 874744

St Ives

- St Ives Leisure Centre
  St Ives Leisure Centre, Trenwith Burrows. Sports facilities and
  fitness activities. 01736 797006

MARTIAL ARTS

Carbis Bay

- Shorin Ryu Karate Club
  www.shorinryukarate.co.uk
  Beginners' courses at Carbis Bay
  Wednesday 7.30-9.30pm (also Connor Downs Womens Institute
  Hall). Male and female instructors in a friendly environment. First
  lesson free. 01736 796636
- Tai Chi (yang form)
  http://www.taichiunion.com Tai Chi Union advanced instructor
  Yang form (also Redruth). Steve Goodyear, 07714 766901

Hayle

- Hayle Judo Kwai
  5-9 years on Tuesday evenings. 10-15 years and 16+ on
  Thursday evenings at The Downes, Foundry Hill, Hayle.
  Sensei Richard, 01736 740723
- Taekwondo
  http://www.firstdefencetaekwondo.co.uk,
  07887 773949 or 07970 329216

Marazion

- Mayoshindo Karate
  Class at Marazion Hall on Tuesdays 7.00 to 8.00pm (juniors) and
  8.00-9.00pm (seniors). Suitable for all levels. First session free.
  Clint, 01736 710296

Penzance

- Grappling Club
  Friday evenings at Penzance YMCA. Matthew Dollins, 01736
  796636; James O'Hanllan, 01736 731828

- Karate
  Sunday class at Penzance YMCA.
  Simon Norris, 01736 796636, enquiries@kynance.com
- Ki Aikido
  http://www.kifederation.co.uk Monday evenings at Humphrey
  Davy School. A complete system of physical and mental
  calmness. Helps to deal with stress and generate wellbeing.
  07720 436812
- Penwith Taoist Arts
  http://www.seahorses.co.uk
  Tai Chi, Feng and Shou kung fu. 01736 785826
- Tai Chi – Qui Gong
  7.00 to 9.00pm classes in Penzance on Tue and Connor Downs
  on Thu. Suitable for all levels.
  John Barber, 01736 754004
- Tai Chi (yang form)
  http://www.taichiunion.com Tai Chi Union advanced instructor
  Yang form (also Redruth).
  Steve Goodyear, 07714 766901

St Just and Lamorna
- Penwith Taoist Arts
  http://www.seahorses.co.uk Tai Chi classes. 01736 785826.

Sennen
- Mayoshindo Karate
  Classes in Sennen at the Community Centre on Fridays, 7.00 to
  8.00pm (junior) and 8.00-9.00pm (senior). Suitable for all levels.
  First session free. Clive, 01736 871664

NATIONAL HEALTH SERVICE

Hospitals
- West Cornwall Hospital, Penzance
  01736 8741139
- Royal Cornwall Hospital,
  Treliske, 01872 250000

NHS
Cornwall and Isles of Scilly

General Practitioners
- Details of your local GP from NHS Direct
  http://www.nhsdirect.nhs.uk 0845 4647

Dental Services
- To access an NHS dentist, 01872 354374 (Long waiting list!)
  Dental Emergency, 01872 354375

Health and Wellbeing

Mental health services

- Community mental health teams for adults suffering from severe mental illness. Available Mon to Fri 8.45am to 5.15pm. Penwith area: 01736 575555

Other Services

- Self Care in Cornwall
  www.cornwallandislesofscilly.nhs.uk/
  CornwallAndIslesOfScillyPCT/InformationForPatients/
  SelfCareinCornwall/SelfCareinCornwall.aspx
  Support available for those with long term conditions and older people.
- Minor Injuries Unit
  Stennack Surgery, St Ives, 01736 793333
  Cambourne-Redruth Hospital, 01209 251777
- NHS Walk-in Centre. The Cardrew Health Centre, Redruth
  Provides easy access to a range of healthcare, advice and specialist services from 8am to 8pm every day of the year.
- Sexual Health, 01872 255044.
  Confidential sexual health advice, tests, and treatment.
- Outlook – Innovation in Psychological Services: www.outlooksw.co.uk
- Eatsome – promoting healthy eating: www.eatsomegoodfood.org
- LeapActive – promoting physical activity for health: www.leapactive.org
- NHS Direct: www.nhsdirect.nhs.uk 0845 4647

Web: www.cornwallandislesofscilly.nhs.uk
Phone: 01726 627 800

PENWITH WALKERS

Health walks on Mon and Thu. Level 1 (45 to 60 min): for those who do little or no physical activity at present and people restricted by mobility problems; Level 2 (60 to 75 min): for people who would like to increase their physical activity

levels and those with minor mobility problems who walk at a moderate speed and are able to cope with moderate gradients; Level 3 (60 to 90 min): for people who already do a certain amount of physical activity and those who walk with a stronger pace and are able to cope with small hills.

Web: http://www.wfh.naturalengland.org.uk/walkfinder/
south-west/penwith-walkers
Email: m.cooper661@btinternet.com
Phone: 07854 232 078

PENZANCE NATURAL HEALTH CENTRE

Opened in 1984 by a group of natural health practitioners to provide a centre where the public could be

assured of a professional approach to complementary medicine. It has had charitable status since 1986 which enables it to provide not only therapy but also a general information service. All their practitioners are qualified and experienced. They also have a large, light and airy room which is used for talks, courses and workshops.

Web: http://www.penzancenaturalhealthcentre.co.uk

Phone: 01736 360 522

Address: 5 Morrab Road, Penzance, Cornwall TR18 4EL

PENZANCE WHEELERS CYCLING CLUB

The PZ Wheelers have a history going back to the 1930s. They hold races and do a 50 to 65 mile ride every Sunday.

Web: www.pzwheelers.co.uk

Email: admin@pzwheelers.co.uk

Phone: 01736 711 363

Address: c/o Mr Mike Tonkin, The Cottage, Plain-An-Gwarry, Marazion, Penzance, Cornwall TR17 0DR

PILATES

Lelant

- Lelant Village Hall. Mon am, Tue eve, Fri am. Kim Hopkins MARH, 01209 831755

Nancledra

- Positive Posture Pilates http://www.p-p-pilates.com Nancledra Mon eve; St Hilary's School Tue eve. Suitable all levels. Alison McSally Hill BA PG Dip, 07906 131726, ajmsally@gmail.com

Penzance

- Rebecca Francis www.pilatesofpenzance.com Small classes after an introductory consultation. Also retreats. 017363 68008 or 079070 600454

PILOT GIG

Cornwall Pilot Gig Association
http://www.cpga.co.uk

Hayle
* Hayle Pilot Gig Rowing Club
http://www.haylegigclub.com
Rowing out of Hayle harbour most Tuesday and Thursday evenings in summer. Competitions, training and 'have a go' too.
haylegigclub@googlemail.com

Marazion
* Mounts Bay Pilot Gig Club
http://www.mountsbaygigclub.org

Pendeen
* Pendeen Pilot Gig Club
http://pendeengig.website.orange.co.uk
All ages over 12 and all abilities. Regular training from Newlyn harbour all year round weather permitting.
Dan Mugglestone, 07866 742987; Geoff and Jill Hoather, 01736 786006; Debs Bassett-Harding, 07739 753327.

Sennen
* Cape Cornwall Pilot Gig Club
http://www.capecornwallgigclub.co.uk
All welcome to social rowing at Sennen harbour. Also training and competitive events.

St Ives
* St Ives Pilot Gig Club
anna@buryanst.freeserve.co.uk

Zennor
* Zennor Pilot Gig Club
http://www.zennorgigclub.com

SIRENS SURF

Traditionally surf schools have been male dominated and focused primarily on the needs of males. Many women of all ages have said that they wish to learn as single gender groups. Often there is less sense of embarrassment, or

pressure of male dominance and this leads to a more relaxed and fun environment. The aim of Sirens Surf is to support women and girls to feel empowered and inspired by their own abilities. To be challenged by what the sea and what Cornwall has to offer in a safe supportive environment. There are small group sessions (maximum 8 females) that give everyone the attention and time that they need.

Web: http://www.sirenssurf.co.uk

Email: sirens.cornwall@gmail.com

Phone: 07815 810 077

ST JOHN AMBULANCE

With thousands of training courses across the country, including Risk Assessment, Fire Marshal, Moving and Handling, and a suite of first

aid courses to suit any training needs, they enable hundreds of thousands of people to protect their colleagues, family, friends, and members of the community.

Web: http://www.sja.org.uk

Address: St John Ambulance Hall, Wendron Street, Helston TR13 8PS

SWIMMING

Hayle

- Hayle Outdoor Pool
www.cornwall.gov.uk
Open during the summer
season. King George Memorial Walk, Phillack, Hayle TR27 5AA
01736 752568

Penzance

- Penzance Leisure Centre
http://www.leisurecentre.com Includes Aquazone, one-to-one lessons, adult swimming lessons and takes GP referrals.
St Clare, Penzance TR18 3QW. 01736 874744
- Penzance Jubilee Pool
http://www.jubileepool.co.uk Open air pool available from May to September. The Promenade, Penzance TR18 4AA
01736 369224, contact@jubileepool.co.uk

St Ives
- St Ives Leisure Centre
  http://www.stives-cornwall.co.uk/stives-leisure-centre.html,
  Trenwith Burrows, St Ives TR26 1HB. 01736 797006

St Just
- Cape Cornwall Golf and Leisure Resort
  http://www.capecornwallgolfclub.co.uk, .com Swimming pool is
  open to the public and available on a pay-as-you-go basis.
  Cape Cornwall Road, St Just, Penzance TR19 7NL,
  01736 788611, enquiries@capecornwall.com

WELCOMING FITNESS

A website for freelance exercise
instructors and dance teachers to
advertise their classes. Look at the
Find Classes page to see what's on.

WelcomingFitness.co.uk

> Web: **http://www.welcomingfitness.co.uk**
>
> Email: **welcomingfitness@gmail.com**
>
> Phone: **01872 865 017**

YOGA

Some of the local yoga classes:

Goldsithney
- Mira Love
  www.miralove.co.uk

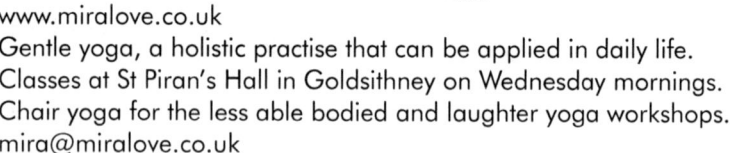

  Gentle yoga, a holistic practise that can be applied in daily life.
  Classes at St Piran's Hall in Goldsithney on Wednesday mornings.
  Chair yoga for the less able bodied and laughter yoga workshops.
  mira@miralove.co.uk

Gulval
- Iyengar Yoga
  Gulval Village Hall, Monday 7.00 to 8.30pm; Thursday 9.30am
  to 11am. Tracy Wearne, 01736 332530

Hayle
- Birthlight Yoga
  www.lovebabyyoga.co.uk
  Toddler, baby and pregnancy yoga classes; and birth rehearsal
  courses at the Passmore Edwards Institute in Hayle.
  Mandy Adams, mandy@lovebabyyoga.co.uk, 07952 836190

- Hatha Yoga
  Classes on Monday evenings and Tuesday and Friday mornings
  at the Passmore Edwards Institute in Hayle.
  Gwynn, 01736 791784 or 07815 945695

Ludgvan

- Judy Van Dop
  Teaches Iyengar Yoga through Penwith College and privately.
  Classes at Ludgvan School. 01736 360880

Newlyn, Penzance etc

- Alexia Hudson
  Iyengar Yoga to improve flexibility, strength, and balance. Classes
  on Monday and Wednesday evenings and Tuesday mornings
  at Newlyn Yoga Studio; Wednesday mornings in Nancledra
  at Gilbert Hall, and Thursday evenings in The Count House,
  Botallack (call to book).
  01736 366313 or 07790 985961, alexiahudson@live.co.uk
- Bimyoga
  http://www.bimyoga.com Gives classes, one-to-one tuition and
  retreats. Belinda Kean, belinda@bimyoga.com, 01736 874966 or
  07833 763806
- Charlie Worthington
  Iyengar Yoga classes at Newlyn Yoga Studio on Wednesday and
  Thursday evening; also leads a meditation open to all on Thursday
  evenings and a gentle restorative yoga class on Friday mornings.
  Classes at The Andrew Hall, Helston on Wednesday evenings.
  01736 363676, charliedharma@hotmail.com
- Indra
  Teaches Power Yoga, a westernised version of Ashtanga Yoga, to
  create energy and vitality. Drop in classes on Friday afternoons at
  Absolute Body Care in Penzance.
  07760 360131 or 367457
- Into Body, Into Being
  Free movement sessions at the Lescudjack Centre in Penzance.
  Playful movement including yoga, Body Psychotherapy, Dance
  and meditation.
  Ellena Fries and Val Stagg, 01736 810409
- Judy Van Dop
  Teaches Iyengar Yoga through Penwith College and privately.
  Classes at Newlyn Yoga Studio, Penwith College. Also classes for
  back pain and a drop in class on Friday afternoons.
  01736 360880

- Kundalini Yoga
  A dynamic blend of asanas, pranayama, mantra, music, and meditation to balance body and mind. Held on Tuesday mornings and Thursday evenings at Archie Browns treatment rooms in Penzance.
  Anna, 07805 674595, annaweschke@hotmail.com
- Leif Olsen
  www.leifolsenyoga.co.uk Teaching focused on breath, flow, and alignment. Offers drop in classes, private tuition, pregnancy yoga and post natal yoga. 01736 787121 or 07877 738494, leifolsenyoga@googlemail.com
- Mira Love
  www.miralove.co.uk Classes at Morrab Surgery in Penzance. See entry under Goldsithney.
- Pamela Masterton
  The Healing Star, 35 Causeway Head, Penzance TR18 2SP, Thursday evening class in Penzance, integral yoga with a meditative approach. Also yoga for mental health.
  01736 330669 or 01736 364454
- Penzance Community Yoga
  Class at the Lescudjack Centre in Penzance, nominal charge. Julie Stone, juliestone1@btinternet.com
- Yoga Nature - Hilary Bell
  www.yoganature.org.uk,
  Qualified occupational therapist registered with BWY and Mandala Yoga Ashram. Gives classes inspired by the Satyananda yoga tradition, Vanda Scaravelli and the Body Mind Centering approach. 07732 527714, hilary@yoganature.org.uk

Sennen, St Buryan and St Just
- Nicolle Fisher, Drop in classes and Private tuition.
  07815 096503, nicollefisher@yahoo.co.uk

St Ives
- Indra
  Teaches Power Yoga, a westernised version of Ashtanga Yoga, to create energy and vitality - a class to suit all ages and abilities on Monday evenings at St Ives Comprehensive school, bookable through Penwith College. 07760 360131
- Ann Nicol
  Iyengar Yoga on Monday mornings at St Ives Library. Work with your body to improve flexibility, strength, co-ordination, and wellbeing. 01736 796248

Heart and Soul

Many questions about the future face us today. Some believe that time and natural resources will run out, others that we'll create solutions. One thing's certain, however: we don't actually *know* what will happen. All we can reliably expect is change. It's important then, that we have a place to explore our mental, emotional and spiritual responses to these uncertainties. Traditionally Church and Chapel have been at the centre of our communities, offering both physical and spiritual support. Today there is also a wide range of other faiths and practices. In addition, a friend's shoulder to cry on or the ear of a confidant at the pub can bring comfort and relief from our confusion and fear. It's somewhat surprising then that we are still arguing and fighting amongst ourselves! The current society values competition and growth over co-operation at any cost. Difference at best is tolerated, at worst attacked. But imagine if our society encountered sudden hardships in the way that Greek society recently has. How would our communities cope? In a precipice transition, religious and spiritual groups would have an important role to play in holding communities together as well as preventing and resolving conflicts. If we want a smooth transition then the onus is on us to make ourselves emotionally and mentally ready for change. We need to build communities that reach beyond religions and beliefs to a sense of neighbourliness regardless of colour or creed. Our God or gods made us stewards of this world and the important thing is mutual respect. Any lasting positive change in the world will need to involve deep changes at the personal and interpersonal level and, wherever we draw inspiration from. Paying attention to our heart and soul can give us the space to prepare for the inevitable problems that will undoubtedly arise.

95

CAMPAIGN FOR NUCLEAR DISARMAMENT

The Campaign for Nuclear Disarmament is an anti-nuclear organisation that advocates unilateral nuclear disarmament by **Campaign** for **Nuclear Disarmament** the United Kingdom, international nuclear disarmament and tighter international arms regulation through agreements such as the Nuclear Non-Proliferation Treaty. It opposes military action that may result in the use of nuclear, chemical or biological weapons and the building of nuclear power stations in the UK. CND was formed in 1957 and has been at the forefront of the peace movement in the UK ever since. Watch out for frequent stalls in Causewayhead, Penzance and the Penzance Peace Festival in Penlee Park.

Web: **http://www.cnduk.org**
Email: **pete@plumpeace.co.uk**
Phone: **01736 787 056**
Address: **Petanna Peace Barn, Carnyorth, Penzance TR19 7QD**

CHOICE CONFLICT RESOLUTION

Conflict Resolution is really just clearer communication. Differing perceptions, difficult personalities and breakdowns in communication often lead to  conflict. Perhaps repeated requests are met with blame, denial, placation and unfulfilled promises. Perhaps we also find it difficult to express our needs to certain people. Learning how to handle our differences and express our needs effectively, can improve our working, family and social environments. Conflict resolution skills help to raise matters directly and effectively without engaging in blame; communicate effectively with difficult personalities; address the reasons for competition and resentment; enhance mutual understanding and co-operative problem-solving. Choice offers tailor-made training, coaching and mediation.

Web: **http://www.choiceconflictresolution.com**

CHURCHES TOGETHER IN PENZANCE AREA

Representatives from Christian Churches and Associations come together and plan joint services of unity, events and activities which

aim to recognise Christian unity - with many activities benefiting all members of the local community. CTIPA is a means of sharing Christian faith and mission through services, events and social activities. These include the CTIPA Breakfast Project which serves breakfast on weekdays to homeless clients; the CTIPA Food Bank which has grown to be an effective service to families in need; and School Assemblies and Chaplaincy work.

Web: http://www.churchestogetherinpenzance.co.uk

CORNISH ANCIENT SITES PROTECTION

Cornish Ancient Sites Protection Network is a charitable partnership formed to look after the ancient sites and monuments of Cornwall. They work closely with local communities and official organisations to protect and promote ancient heritage landscape through research, education and outreach activities. Every year they organise a weekend called Pathways to the Past which consists of walks and talks amongst the ancient sites of West Penwith. This event has become a popular one for locals and visitors alike.

Web: http://www.cornishancientsites.com
Email: info@cornishancientsites.com
Phone: 01736 787 186
Address: Whitewaves, Boscaswell, Pendeen, Penzance TR19 7EP

CORNWALL ANCIENT TREE FORUM

The Ancient Tree Forum (ATF) and the Woodland Trust work together to promote the conservation of ancient trees. The Ancient Tree

97

Forum was founded in 1993 by a group of people who had come together to discuss the management of ancient trees. It was subsequently one of the key partners in English Nature's Veteran Trees Initiative. Cornwall's Great Tree Hunt is part of the three-year 'Great Trees Project' to safeguard the future of Cornwall's ancient and significant trees and anyone can get involved.

Web: **http://www.ancient-tree-forum.org.uk**
Email: **forestry@cornwall.gov.uk**
Phone: **01872 222 000**

HEARTSONG CEREMONIES

Heartsong Ceremonies delivers individually tailored ceremonies for weddings, civil partnerships, handfastings, namings, blessings, anniversaries, funerals,  memorials and all special events. All beliefs, values and aspects of spirituality (or none) are honored. You can be as creative or as traditional as you wish, choosing the length of the ceremony, the venue (inside or outside) and all the elements of the ceremony itself. Danu Fox can deliver as much or as little of the ceremony as you wish and you can be supported to lead/ deliver as you choose. She is a trained independent celebrant and can design and deliver all aspects of ceremony and ritual. Ceremonies are not just for individuals, couples and families but also for groups of friends, community groups and public or corporate bodies. Ceremony can be magical, life changing and full of integrity.

Web: **http://www.heartsongceremonies.co.uk**
Email: **info@heartsongceremonies.co.uk**
Phone: **01736 786 267**
Address: **New Cottage, Boswedden, St Just, Penzance TR19 7NJ**

MEYN MAMVRO

Meyn Mamvro is the magazine of ancient stones and sacred sites in Cornwall. It has been published

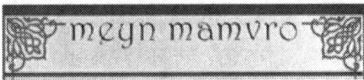

regularly 3 times a year since 1986, and, taken together, all the editions contain a wealth of original material about the prehistory and ancient customs of Cornwall. Meyn Mamvro Publications also produce a number of books and booklets about the ancient sites of Cornwall.

> Web: **http://www.meynmamvro.co.uk**

MINDFULNESS CORNWALL

Mindfulness Cornwall is a group of dedicated, committed, and trained practitioners who are delivering mindfulness in a variety of settings across Cornwall. They offer a

Mindfulness Cornwall

range of mindfulness based approaches including 8 week courses, training days, mindful yoga and one-to-one mindfulness based therapy. People take part to promote general well-being; reduce stress, anxiety and panic; cope with low mood or depression; and deal with conditions such as chronic fatigue, chronic pain, fibromyalgia, high blood pressure, sleep disorder and headaches.

> Web: **http://mindfulnesscornwall.co.uk**
> Email: **contact@mindfulnesscornwall.co.uk**

PARALLEL COMMUNITY

The Parallel Community is a network linking people and groups across the world. It's about expressing

and developing a positive contribution for change - human, social, ecological, creative, commercial and spiritual. It's a mutual support network and resource for people and groups working to build a new and better world. It's a container and channel, a forum for ideas, a skills-exchange and a friendship family. The Parallel Community started in Penwith and the network is spreading everywhere, across borders both national and of the mind and heart.

> Web: **http://www.parallelcommunity.com**
> Address: **PO Box 11, Hayle, Cornwall TR27 6YF**

Heart and Soul

SACRED FIRE COMMUNITY

Long before the fluorescing flicker of technology, people would spend their evenings gathered around the Fire. They shared the stories that gave life meaning, they felt a deep  sense of connection to each other, nature, and Divine. The Sacred Fire Community is relatively young in its current form. It began in the USA in the mid-1990s but in a relatively short space of time it has begun to spark interest around the world. The Fire Circles are at the centre of it all: Today, the Sacred Fire Community sponsors some 75 regular Community Fires in North America, the United Kingdom, Australia, and across the world. The nearest one is held every month just outside Hayle.

Web: **http://www.sacredfirecommunity.org**
Email: **mjlocke@hotmail.com**

WHITECROSS BUDDHIST CENTRE

The Whitecross Buddhist Centre is located between Penzance and St Erth. It is run by a group of individuals from various Buddhist traditions (including Therevada,  Zen and Mahayana) who meet regularly to practice meditation together and to share their thoughts and understandings. They welcome anyone who is interested in joining the weekly group meditation sessions.

Web: **http://www.whitecrossbuddhistcentre.moonfruit.com**
Email: **lee.stevenson2@tiscali.co.uk**
Phone: **01736 763 623**
Address: **Gilly Lane, Whitecross, Penzance, Cornwall TR20 8BZ**

Manufacture and Craft

While oil is cheap, it's inevitable that a lot of the goods we buy will be manufactured in far away places where wage levels are much lower. The other side of the coin is that local manufacture will only (currently) be viable for high value, mostly luxury products. This is in sharp focus in Penwith where so many livelihoods depend on tourist spending on craft goods. Increased energy costs over time are likely to mean that imported goods will once again became prohibitively expensive. However, in that circumstance, the UK is unlikely to be in a position to quickly rebuild its mass manufacturing infrastructure which has been almost completely eradicated in the last 30 years. The result: reduced availability of goods. But there is a silver lining: small-scale local manufacture could once again come to the fore and this is something which gives much satisfaction to a lot of people. Could we start making a smooth transition to this more sustainable existence now? It would mean building up manufacturing skills locally but for this to be viable now it would have to be, initially, for the craft goods market. The subtle difference is that an eye needs to be cast to the future whenever equipment or skills are being acquired. Every time the question asked should be: "Could this be re-used in the manufacture of more everyday goods? Could it be done without electricity or fossil fuel?" If we can afford it as individuals, we *must* financially support craftspeople who have this attitude – particularly those who are gaining skills that might be essential in the future (eg blacksmithing). We need to stop putting all our eggs in one basket and come up with multiple solutions for the future – building up skills, tools and knowledge of local raw materials in the process.

ART OF HEALING

Windrose Morris produces small batches of handmade herbal creams. She and husband Dylan try to grow most of the herbs themselves and are now able to 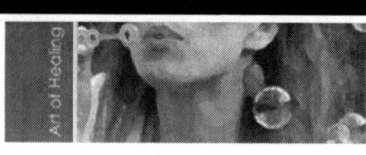 use some of their own honey and bees wax as well. She sells these creams at farmers markets, craft events and from her website.

Web: http://www.artofhealing.org.uk

Email: windrosemorris@gmail.com

Phone: 01736 333 927

CORNISH LIME COMPANY

Building lime, limewash and paint pigments. The Cornish Lie Company manufacture in Cornwall but use Derbyshire limestone. They  make a completely natural cement, fast setting, called Prompt and sell this all over the country for renovating old buildings. They also make Hemsulate, an insulation made from hemp and a lime binder.

Web: http://www.cornishlime.co.uk

Phone: 01208 797 790

Address: Brims Park, Old Callywith Road, Bodmin PL31 2DZ

CORNISH ORGANIC WOOL

Cornish Organic Wool comes from certified organic farms and is spun by a certified spinning mill and dyed on site - all within the county of Cornwall. All processes are done  to strict Soil Association standards so the result is organic wool with a truly tiny eco footprint. One of the Cornish Wool farmers is in Zennor. Purchase online or from Knit Wits (see page 104).

Web: http://www.cornishorganicwool.co.uk

Email: info@cornishorganicwool.co.uk

Phone: 01736 350 905

Address: King's Cott, Boswarthen, Newbridge, Penzance TR28 8PA

Manufacture and Craft

CORNISH WILLOW

They handcraft all their products (rustic garden furniture, willow baskets etc) in Cornwall using, as far as possible, locally sourced and home grown materials.

Web: http://cornishwillow.co.uk

Phone: 01566 782 626

Address: Green View, Middlewood, North Hill, Launceston PL15 7NN

CORNISH WOOLS

They produce, market and sell their own exclusive range of sustainable and biodegradable knitting wools made from the fleece of sheep, alpacas and goats that are reared and farmed in Cornwall. Cornish Artisan is produced by them in their Perranuthnoe dye workshop – it's a range of yarns dyed using mostly natural dyes.

Web: http://www.cornishwools.co.uk

Email: info@cornishwools.co.uk

Phone: 01736 711 288

Address: Lynfield Craft Centre, Perranuthnoe, Penzance TR20 9NE

CORNWALL POULTRY HOUSES

Cornwall Poultry Houses offer top quality chicken houses, chicken runs, duck houses and poultry equipment. All their products are designed for easy management and manoeuvrability. They are hand built by a local craftsman from tanalised timber (from sustainable sources) and covered with 19mm tanalised shiplap.

Web: http://www.cornwallpoultryhouses.co.uk

Email: shop@cornwallpoultryhouses.co.uk

Phone: 01736 787 283

Address: Drycarne House, Higher Tregerest, Newbridge TR20 8PY

Manufacture and Craft

JEAN BARRY SOAP COMPANY

The company was founded by Jean Barry, an expert in complementary therapies with a belief in caring for and nurturing both ourselves and the environment. The company

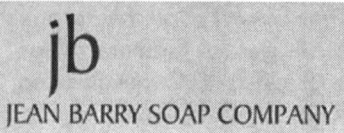

promotes these beliefs by manufacturing products made entirely from natural ingredients and purely in Cornwall. The traditional cold process uses no detergents, only vegetable oils combined with lye and water. Once they have been stored to allow them to mature, the soaps are hand polished, before being displayed in the Penzance shop for sale to the public.

Web: http://www.jbsoap.co.uk

Phone: 01736 361 888

Address: 25 Causewayhead, Penzance, Cornwall TR18 2SP

KNIT WITS

Knit Wits Wool and Yarn Shop is one of the foremost wool stockists in the south-west and is well known for stocking Cornish organic wool; based in Penzance it is owned and

run by Julia Hopson. They have an online store as well.

Web: http://www.knitwitspenzance.co.uk

Phone: 01736 367 069

Address: 45, Causewayhead, Penzance, Cornwall TR18 2SS

KUIAMA CRAFTS

This is the only outlet for Mowhay Wool made from sheep at the Kehelland Farm, Camborne and spun in Launceston.

Web: http://www.kuiamacrafts.com

Email: heidi_moore@btconnect.com

Phone: 01736 798 009

Address: 42 Fore Street, St Ives, Cornwall TR26 1HE

LIN LOVEKIN

Lin makes a variety of baskets using Somerset and homegrown Cornish willow (commissions considered). She also teaches beginners basketmaking workshops throughout West Cornwall. Small groups with lots of individual attention.

Web: **http://www.linlovekinbaskets.co.uk**

Phone: **01736 763 676**

Address: **Carleen, Helston, Cornwall TR13 9NW**

NATURAL FIBRE COMPANY

This company spins and dyes wool helping local farmers to generate greater income from their flocks. They are now providing dyed wool, carefully toned to compliment the natural fibre colours.

Phone: **01566 777 635**

Web: **www.thenaturalfibre.co.uk**

Email: **info@thenaturalfibrecompany.co.uk**

Address: **Unit B Pipers Court, Pennygillam Way, Launceston, Cornwall PL15 7PJ**

RAWNSLEY WOOD PRODUCTS

Tino Rawnsley offers many products including fencing, garden furniture and firewood made with timber from local woodlands. Also services such as hedge laying and woodland management. He gives demonstrations of charcoal making and training in areas of woodland management and ecology.

Web: **http://www.cornishwoodland.co.uk**

Phone: **01208 813 490**

Address: **Waverley, Burlawn, Wadebridge, Cornwall PL27 7LD**

Manufacture and Craft

RUNWATER SHOES

Phil Runwater has been making footwear and accessories since the 1980s. All footwear is handmade using the finest leathers and components. Most are made to measure although he does carry some stock.

Web: http://www.runwatershoes.co.uk

Phone: 01872 552 404

Address: Trevaunance Cove Workshops, Quay Road, St Agnes, Cornwall TR5 0RS

Manufacture and Craft

SMYTHICK FORGE

Lisa Harrison creates a range of interior hardware, artistic ironwork and contemporary jewellery in her forge, near Falmouth. She continues to teach Blacksmithing Workshops and participated in a 'Living History' project with Cape Cornwall school children. She regularly demonstrates and exhibits her work at local design fairs, contemporary craft shows and agricultural shows.

SMYTHICK FORGE

Web: http://www.smythickforge.co.uk

Address: Trevone Quarry, Mabe Burnthouse, Penryn TR10 9JQ

TREE-CYCLED

Tree-cycled is a new business operating from near Newbridge. It is responding to the need to remove diseased Rhododendrons by producing charcoal out of this

otherwise wasted resource. In addition they produce Top-Bar (bee-friendly) beehives and yurts, squirts (camping yurts) and raw-fleece bed mats which are ideal for the traveller. Where possible they're using recycle materials to make their products.

Web: http://tree-cycled.weebly.com

Money and Livelihood

We've all been taught at an impressionable age that "Money makes the World go round". Apparently the more money you have the happier you'll be. And the way to get money is to work. You'll be an "upstanding" member of society with a proper job and a "nice" house. Those who don't get this message are left with much lower incomes, benefits and the dream of winning the lottery. The actual idea of working to provide security for ourselves and our families is perfectly reasonable and the actual doing of work is important to many. But not everybody loves their work and a lot of excessive consumption happens because people feel that they *deserve* to consume all sorts of things as a reward for the misery of their daily 9 to 5. In addition so many of our jobs are dependent on a system which is predicated on growth – a model that is looking increasingly unsustainable. As it becomes less viable many people will lose work and access to benefits will also decline. What would you do if you were made redundant? Could you see it as an opportunity to invent a different work-life balance? Proper jobs can end quickly whereas a so-called "portfolio" career (carrying out many kinds of tasks, some for money, some for free, some via a local economic trading scheme, some via a local currency) goes on forever. The person locked away in a "proper job" is very much more vulnerable on the day that there's a run on the banks than the portfolio person who can draw on the social wealth in their reservoir of gratitude (and possibly savings in the local credit union). You and your family might have less money. But look at it this way: you go to work to earn money to pay people to do things you don't have the time to do (or learn how to do) yourself because you're at work! If you spend less money you're effectively earning time and this can be very useful indeed!

THE CO-OPERATIVE BANK

Since 1872 the Co-operative Bank has been providing responsible banking, insurance and investment advice to customers and members.

The co-operative bank

Being owned by a co-op, they're accountable to members and customers, not shareholders. The Co-operative Bank branch network is much smaller than other banks but their merger with Britannia Building Society means that they now have additional branches across the country at which basic banking services can be carried out. It's also possible to use their UK-based call centres and website. The nearest current full branch is in Plymouth but there is a Britannia branch in Truro.

Web: **http://www.co-operativebank.co.uk**
Phone: **01872 273 573**
Address: **Britannia, 7-8 St Nicholas Street, Truro TR1 2RL**

CORNISH COMMUNITY BANKING

CCB is working to provide a real alternative to the High Street banks. It is a local Credit Union working for the people of Cornwall. They want to bring a

cornish community banking

fresh approach to the work of the credit unions offering a range of services like the new Credit Union Current Account which allows more accessible banking and easy access to members' pay, benefits and savings. They have weekly sessions in Penzance and Newlyn - see their own website for details.

Web: **http://www.cornishcommunitybanking.co.uk**
Phone: **0800 055 6873**
Email: **ccbadmin@cornishcommunitybanking.co.uk**
Address: **11a Frances Street, Truro, Cornwall TR1 3DN**

Money and Livelihood

ECOLOGY BUILDING SOCIETY

When you place your savings with the Ecology Building Socoety you help to fund mortgages that lead to a more sustainable

future. And if you have plans for a property or project that will improve our shared environment, take a look at their mortgages first. They like to lend on: Energy efficient housing, Ecological renovation, Derelict and dilapidated properties, Small-scale and ecological enterprise and Low-impact lifestyles. By opening a savings account with the Ecology you are helping to build a more sustainable future. You receive a return on savings and are also creating a fund to advance on even more sustainable properties and projects.

Web: **http://www.ecology.co.uk**
Phone: **0845 674 5566**
Email: **info@ecology.co.uk**
Address: **7 Belton Road, Silsden, Keighley, West Yorkshire BD20 0EE**

PENWITH LETS

Penzance LETS functioned for many years but is sadly no more. Penwith LETS (Local Exchange Trading Scheme) will carry on the tradition - helping people exchange services with other people in the community

without the need for money. The group will be run by and for local people, creating wealth that stays in the area. It puts people in touch with a thriving social network and a great variety of resources and skills. LETS is a way of helping people to help themselves. Everybody has skills and someone out there needs yours!

Web: **http://www.penwithlets.org.uk**
Email: **info@penwithlets.org.uk**

Money and Livelihood

TRIODOS BANK

Triodos offers you the opportunity to save for a sustainable future. They have a range of personal savings accounts but, whichever you choose, your money will earn interest. However, Triodos will only use your money in positive ways, supporting people and organisations whose aim is to make the world a better place – socially, culturally and environmentally. They lend money to a huge range of people and organisations (and have lent to at least one project in Penwith). Every loan application is assessed on its merits and they're proud of their record of successfully backing businesses other commercial lenders don't always understand.

Triodos ⊛ Bank

Web: **http://www.triodos.co.uk**

Phone: **0800 328 2181**

Address: **Brunel House, 11 The Promenade, Bristol BS8 3NN**

COAST

Coast are an independent body and a social enterprise, not core funded, based in a refurbished barn in Cornwall. All their income comes from contract work for private companies, local authorities and other organisations that they work with. They encourage, inform, network, research, lobby, measure, persuade, object, question, bend ears, break boundaries and never knowingly give up!

Web: **http://www.coastproject.co.uk**

Phone: **01872 562 057**

Email: **info@coastproject.co.uk**

Address: **Penstraze Business Centre, Truro, Cornwall TR4 8HY**

Money and Livelihood

KABIN

Kabin promote co-operative solutions and provide well-informed, high quality support to groups and individuals interested in co-ops and social

enterprises. They encourage, promote, develop, and support community led and/or community owned solutions - particularly those that pertain to the health of local economies. Kabin is working with The Co-operative Enterprise Hub to bring you advice, training and consultancy on how to set up, run and grow a sustainable co-operative business. You can apply for up to four days support which includes business planning, financial, staffing, legal and governance advice.

Web: **http://kernowkabin.wordpress.com**
Phone: **01872 262 259**
Email: **coopdevelopment@gmail.com**
Address: **3 Trenhaile Terrace, Malpas, Truro, Cornwall TR1 1SL**

LOCAL LOYALTY CARDS

Hayle
- Hayle Chamber of Commerce
  http://www.haylechamber.org.uk

Penzance
- Penzance Town Council and Penzance Chamber of Commerce
  http://www.penzance.co.uk/loyaltycard

St Ives
- St Ives Chamber of Trade and Commerce
  http://stiveschamber.co.uk

SCHOOL FOR SOCIAL ENTREPRENEURS

SSE Cornwall is an initiative of a coalition of organisations who've come together to bring the social entrepreneurial approach

and methodology to the South-West. They exist to provide training and opportunities to enable people and companies to use their creative and entrepreneurial abilities more fully for social benefit. Cornwall SSE supports individuals to set up new charities, social enterprises and social businesses across Cornwall and the Isles of Scilly.

Web: **http://www.sse.org.uk/school.php?schoolid=7**
Phone: **07530 262 430**
Email: **cornwall@sse.org.uk**
Address: **Room 233, One Stop Shop, Penwinnick Road, St Austell, Cornwall PL25 5DR**

WEST CORNWALL LOCAL ACTION GROUP

West Cornwall Local Action Group has established grant funds for projects which improve the rural economy, build enterprise or which improve the quality of life in rural west Cornwall. The Group covers areas which were the districts of Penwith and Kerrier except for Camborne, Pool and Redruth. The focus for grant aid is for projects in the rural area or where the project benefits people from the rural area.

The four priorities are: to stimulate rural innovation and enhance access to the environment; to encourage the provision of bespoke rural workspace and build enterprise in rural areas; to improve quality of life and access to learning opportunities in rural areas; and to derive sustainable socio-economic benefits from rural tourism activities. The Small Grants Scheme operates in two areas: Small Community Projects (total value of less than £30,000, may apply for grant aid to support community initiatives identified in the community plans such as Parish Plans or Market and Coastal Town Initiative Plans); Small Grants for Business (grant scheme open to new or developing micro businesses and social enterprises with less than ten employees).

Web: **http://www.localactioncornwall.info**
Phone: **01209 611 116**
Email: **clare.leverton@cornwalldevelopmentcompany.co.uk**

Transport and Communications

Moving people and goods around costs a lot of energy. In the past it was free wind energy powering sailing ships that made Penwith less isolated than it might otherwise have been. Plentiful supplies of liquid fuel have made physical transportation seem like something that can be done without thought. But as oil supplies diminish then it will become relatively more expensive once again. People's horizons have been widened by cheaper transportation and that is a really good thing but the mindset that says that we can go where we want when we want will be no more. Those on lower incomes are already affected by this but it will eventually spread to most people. It's obvious that – for many journeys – public transport can make the same fuel go a lot further than if it were used in numerous private vehicles. So why don't more people use it? Once again it's cheap oil distorting everything. The economics of vehicle ownership are such that there are high fixed costs – once you've paid these you're drawn in so far financially already that it often is cheaper to drive than take the bus or train. Passenger numbers drop off substantially and fares have to rise to make services financially viable. This results in public transport seeming expensive and consequently less attractive. So what can we do to be part of a transition in transport if it's this difficult to take action today? If you have a vehicle then, most importantly, notice the choices that you're making. Is your journey really necessary? Could you, instead, make use of the electronic communication infrastructure that we now have (Skype conferencing etc)? If you do decide to drive then plan your journeys for the optimum use of fuel, join one of the lift-sharing schemes and from time-to-time, at least, get used to taking the bus!

CAR SHARE CORNWALL - LIFTSHARE

Cornwall Council has worked in partnership with other local authorities and the national LiftShare organisation. It aims to  maximise people's travel options whilst also reducing the number of cars on the roads. The website is designed to assist you in contacting potential lift-sharing partners and gives you the ability to limit your search according to your own requirements. It allows people to benefit from the convenience of the car, whilst alleviating the associated problems of cost, congestion and pollution. If you have specific requirements, such as, only wishing to travel with a member of the same sex you can limit your search that way. You may also wish to use it as a member of a private group or public group. This way you can restrict your search to fellow members of your group or those linked to it.

> **Web: http://www.carsharecornwall.com**
>
> **Email: support@liftshare.com**
>
> **Phone: 08700 111 199**

THE CORNISH WAY

The Cornish Way is a project developed by the Cornwall Council Countryside Service, in partnership with Sustrans. Starting at the  county boundary near Bude, its six inter-linking trails for cyclists and walkers pass through towns and villages as they make their way through Cornwall's distinctive countryside to Land's End. Certain off-road routes are also accessible to equestrians and the mobility-impaired. With mainly minor and rural road and traffic-free, off-road routes there are opportunities for new or novice cyclists as well as some challenging routes for the more experienced. Even if you don't have your own bike, you can hire one for the day. The Cornish Way forms a major part of National Route 3 of the National Cycle Network. Within Penwith it runs from Hayle and ends at Lands End. On the way it passes through St Erth, Crowlas, Long Rock, Penzance, Newlyn, Mousehole, Lamorna, St Buryan and Sennen Cove.

> **Web: http://www.cornwall.gov.uk/default.aspx?page=13405**

CORNWALL RAMBLERS

The Penwith and Kerrier group covers the area from Portreath on the north-west coast, west to Land's End, easterly along the south coast, around the Lizard peninsula and  up to and including the Helford river estuary. The landscape is varied with the coast path, beaches, harbours, archaeological sites, old mining sites, open moors and hidden valleys. They have a walk at least once a week all year round led by local leaders.

Web: **http://www.cornwallramblers.org.uk**

Email: **sylvronan@btinternet.com**

Phone: **01736 740 542**

Address: **c/o Mrs Sylvia Ronan, Trebant, Ludgvan Churchtown, Penzance, Cornwall TR20 8HH**

CROSS COUNTRY

Arriva's train operating company operates a network of express and long-distance train services between  a variety of towns and cities outside London. These include the route from Aberdeen to Penzance.

Web: **http://www.crosscountrytrains.co.uk**

Address: **XC Trains Limited, Admiral Way, Doxford Int. Business Park, Sunderland SR3 3XP**

THE CYCLE CENTRE

They stock a wide range of mountain bikes, road bikes, electric bikes and BMX. In addition they carry an extensive range of components, clothing and accessories: from panniers and rack bags to lights and helmets.

Web: **http://cyclecentre.net**

Email: **bikes@cyclecentre.net**

Phone: **01736 351 671**

Address: **1 New Street, Penzance, Conwall TR18 2LZ**

Transport and Communications

ECO DRIVE

Eco-drive was formed to give people the choice of using Electric Vehicles. Electric vehicles are often a viable alternative for many private motorists and commercial
operations but have been under-promoted in the UK. Eco-drive is not 'pro-car' but they are being realistic. People will continue to use cars so where possible these should have as low an impact as possible. The key is safe, reliable and convenient recharging. Charging Stations for EVs are the equivalent of filling station fuel pumps for conventional vehicles. Usually these will be used at the vehicle's normal 'home' or base, but may be in other locations. Eco-drive is partnering with Cornwall Council for Cornwall to become one of the UK's first 'Plugged In Places'. The aim is to provide a network of around 400 charging stations across Cornwall for, initially, a public sector fleet and subsequently private users and tourists.

Web: **http://www.eco-drive.co.uk**
Email: **info@eco-drive.co.uk**
Phone: **0845 466 3835**
Address: **PO Box 255, Penzance, Cornwall TR18 9AA**

FIRST BUS

First Bus run many of the local services within Penwith and Cornwall, including the following:

1/1A	Penzance - Newlyn - St Buryan - Land's End (some journeys operated by Western Greyhound)
2	Penzance - Marazion - Porthleven - Helston
2A	Penzance - Porthleven - Helston - Penryn - Falmouth
5	Penzance - Newlyn - Gwavas
6	Penzance - Newlyn - Mousehole
10/10A	Penzance - St Just
11	Pendennis Rd - Manor Way - Treneere (Penzance Circ)
14	St Ives - Hayle - Camborne - Redruth - Truro
16	Penzance - Nancledra - St Ives

17/17A,B	Penzance - Carbis Bay - St Ives
18	Penzance - Hayle - Camborne - Redruth - Truro
X18	Penzance - Hayle - Truro
300	Penwith Circular - Penzance, St Ives and Lands End (Good Friday to end September)
302	Penzance - Praa Sands (June to September)

Web: **http://www.firstgroup.com/ukbus/devon_cornwall**
Phone: **0845 600 1420**
Address: **The Ride, Chelson Meadow, Plymouth, Devon PL9 7JT**

FIRST GREAT WESTERN

First Great Western operates
high speed, commuter, regional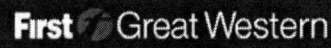
and branch line train services,
covering London, South Wales, the West of England and Devon
and Cornwall. It runs Inter City services from Penzance as well as
local services to and from Carbis Bay, Hayle, Lelant, Lelant Saltings,
Penzance, St Erth and St Ives.

Web: **http://www.firstgreatwestern.co.uk**
Phone: **08457 000 125**
Address: **Customer Services Team,**
Freepost SWB40576, Plymouth, Devon PL4 6ZZ

HAYLE CYCLES

Hayle Cycles describe themselves
as a real local bike shop. They are
situated in the centre of St Ives Bay
and a few minutes from the Towans
beaches. You can buy a bicycle, hire a bicycle or have your bike
serviced. They also offer spare parts and friendly advice.

Web: **http://www.haylecycles.com**
Email: **haylecycles@postmaster.co.uk**
Phone: **01736 753 825**
Address: **36 Penpol Terrace, Hayle, Cornwall TR27 4BQ**

HELSTON RAILWAY PRESERVATION

Until 1962 the Helston branch line linked Gwinear Road on the Cornish Main Line to Helston. The line was surveyed in 1994 in order to conduct a feasibility study into its reopening.

It was decided that due to the amount of work needed and the possible revenue that could be generated, it was not worth the effort and the idea was eventually dropped. In 2005 volunteers from the Helston Railway Preservation Company started work on restoring a section of the line at Trevarno Gardens. By 2012 a mile of track had been completed and plans to rebuild Truthall Station were well advanced.

Web: **http://www.helstonrailway.co.uk**

Email: **membership@helstonrailway.co.uk**

Address: **Trevarno Manor, Crowntown, Helston TR13 0RU**

ISLES OF SCILLY TRAVEL

Formed in 1920 and set up by the inhabitants of the Islands with the aim of providing regular, cost effective and enjoyable travel between the mainland and the Isles of Scilly. It runs the Scillonian passenger ferry between May and October; year round freight services; Lands End Airport and (since 1984) the Skybus commercial passenger flights.

Web: **http://www.islesofscilly-travel.co.uk**

Phone: **0845 710 5555**

Address: **Isles of Scilly Travel Centre, Quay St, Penzance TR18 4BZ**

LANDS END CYCLE HIRE

Lands End Cycle Hire are based in Trewellard and can provide you with a bike for use on the Penwith peninsula, anywhere west of the A30 between Penzance and St Ives all the way to Lands End. You can park at Trewellard and bike along the B3306 to explore the Mining Heritage area, or they can bring the bikes to you. You can also hire their bikes from Lodey Sails, Long Rock, Penzance TR20 9TT.

Web: **http://www.landsendcyclehire.co.uk**
Email: **info@landsendcyclehire.co.uk**
Phone: **0788 545 2997**
Address: **Unit 3D, Trewellard Industrial Estate, Trewellard, Penzance, Cornwall TR19 7TF**

PASTY CONNECTION

If you're a member of Facebook then you can join this group. It's a place where people from West Penwith can post when they intend to travel up the line and also  back in the other direction from, for instance, London or Bristol. Passengers might like to offer to share fuel costs and/or the driving.

Web: **https://www.facebook.com/groups/123436594346182/**

PENWITH ACCESS AND RIGHTS OF WAY

PAROW was formed in 2002 and is a partnership supported by Cornwall Council. Its object is to promote and achieve wider access to public rights of way,  paths and open land in Penwith, with further development of the network, in partnership with all aspects of the community. PAROW Forum meetings are held once each month. All interested in paths and rights of way are welcome to attend. PAROW employs a Paths Officer and Assistant Path Officer to work alongside Cornwall Council, Parish Councils and their agents.

Web: **http://www.parow.org.uk**
Email: **secretary@parow.org.uk**
Phone: **01736 811 124**

PUBLIC TRANSPORT IN CORNWALL

This is the Cornwall Public Transport Information website. It's designed to provide full timetable information on all bus services  operating in Cornwall, as well as information on rail, coach, air and ferry services.

> **Web:** http://www.cornwallpublictransport.info
> **Email:** ptu@cornwall.gov.uk
> **Phone:** 03001 234 222
> **Address:** Passenger Transport Unit - Cornwall Council, County Hall, Truro, Cornwall TR1 3AY

ST MICHAEL'S WAY

St Michael's Way was thought to have been used by pilgrims, missionaries and travellers, 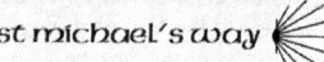 especially those from Ireland and Wales, to avoid crossing the treacherous waters around Land's End. It may date back to pre-historic times (10,000BCE - 410CE). The trail stretches 19.5km from Lelant to Marazion. St Michael's Way has been developed with the guidance of the Bredereth Sen Jago (Cornish Pilgrims of St James) and the Cornish Bureau for European Relations.

> **Web:** http://www.cornwall.gov.uk/default.aspx?page=13233

SUSTRANS

Sustrans makes smarter travel choices possible, desirable and inevitable. They're a leading UK charity enabling people to travel  by foot, bike or public transport for more of the journeys that they make every day. Sustrans works with families, communities, policy-makers and partner organisations so that people are able to choose healthier, cleaner and cheaper journeys, with better places and spaces to move through and live in. National Route 3 of the National Cycle Network connects Land's End in Cornwall to Bristol via St Austell, Bude, Barnstaple, Taunton and Wells. The route is fully open and signed, though improvements are still planned to create more traffic-free route options along the way.

Web: **http://www.sustrans.org.uk/what-we-do national-cycle-network/route-numbering-system/42**
Phone: **0117 926 8893**
Address: **2 Cathedral Square, College Green, Bristol BS1 5DD**

WEST PENWITH COMMUNITY BUS ASSOCIATION

West Penwith Community Bus has been in service since 1985. They mainly operate a demand and response service known as Dial-a-Ride which offers a flexible pick up and drop off point and, wherever possible, a door to door service. This service offers transport in the West Penwith area and covers nine villages in the surrounding rural area. The Association is run by a voluntary committee and employs a part-time administrator and six part-time drivers. They are a non-profit making organisation which, in the main, provides transport to people who would otherwise have no access to transport, have difficulty in using public transport, are students, aged over 60 or who have difficulty in walking. Buses are equipped with wheelchair access and assistance dogs travel free of charge.

Web: **http://www.wp-communitybus.co.uk**
Email: **wpcombus@lafrowda.wanadoo.co.uk**
Phone: **0845 201 1359**
Address: **The Lafrowda Club, 3 Chapel Street, St Just, Penzance, Cornwall TR19 7LS**

Transport and Communications

WESTERN GREYHOUND

Western Greyhound is a locally-based, family-run business that has **westerngreyhound** been operating since 1998. They run an extensive bus network throughout Cornwall and into Devon including the following local routes:

501 Penzance - St Buryan - Porthcurno - Land's End
504 Penzance - St Buryan - Land's End - St Just
507 St Just - Pendeen - Gurnard's Head
508 Penzance - Zennor - Gurnard's Head - St Ives
509 Penzance - Sancreed - St Just
512 Alverton - Lansdowne Estate (Penzance Circular)
513 Penzance - Marazion - Leedstown
515 Penzance - Hayle - Gwithian
547 St Ives - Hayle - Perranporth - Newquay

Web: **http://www.westerngreyhound.com**
Email: **info@westerngreyhound.com**
Phone: **01637 871 871**
Address: **Western House, St Austell Street, Summercourt, Newquay, Cornwall TR8 5DR**

HAYLE PUMP NEWSLETTER

The Hayle Pump is published every other month and they welcome contributions from Hayle and immediately surrounding areas. They need: articles, humour, cartoons, information, what's on, letters, adverts. They are always  looking for help in the following areas: collecting advertising, delivering the printed Pump, writing, editing, proofreading, calling around to get material, desktop publishing and working with printers.

Web: **http://www.haylepump.org.uk**
Email: **editor@haylepump.org.uk**
Address: **Passmore Edwards Inst, 13-15 Hayle Trc, Hayle TR27 4BU**

DIGITAL PENINSULA NETWORK

Open from Monday to Friday with full disability access. Downstairs@ DPN ... there are PC and Mac workstations. Access to Internet Area, equipped with existing machines,  broadband, MS Office and possibly open source software. Scanning, black and white printing, copying, faxing and technical Support. Upstairs@DPN ... video editing and spacious area used for training opportunities. All training and meeting spaces, the video-editing suite and equipment hire must be booked (and paid for where necessary) in advance and is subject to availability. Also high quality printing and photocopying, faxing, laminating, binding, outgoing telephone calls and general office sundries. Technical support available at the centre.

Web: http://www.digitalpeninsula.com

Email: office@digitalpeninsula.com

Phone: 01736 333 700

Address: 1 & 2 Old Brewery Yard, Bread St, Penzance TR18 2SL

PENWITH RADIO

Penwith Community Radio is a social company with a board of directors. The station has a manager who is supported by a team of volunteers who have trained in a wide range of media skills including presenting, editing, recording, office management, technical development, programme making and journalism. There is a wide range of output covering community issues, arts and specialist music programmes. The station is committed to all aspects of social inclusion and environmental sustainability. The community radio aims to encourage the personal development of volunteers and to respond to the concerns of people in the Penwith area. Broadcasting is currently via the internet but they've recently been awarded a full FM licence.

Web: http://penwithradio.co.uk

Phone: 01736 362 884

Address: Wharfside Shopping Centre, Market Jew St, Penzance, Cornwall TR18 2GB

Transport and Communications

THE PHONE CO-OP

The Phone Co-op is the only co-operative which offers phone, broadband and mobile services. They are owned by their members

thePhoneCo‑op

- a group of people united by shared values, shared ownership and democratically made decisions. You can become one of those members and then you can have a say in how the business is run. They are socially responsible and aim to be 'good neighbours'. They are proving that it is possible to run a successful business while behaving ethically and with a sense of social responsibility - they're thinking long-term.

Web: **http://www.thephone.coop**

Phone: **0845 458 9000**

Address: **5 The Millhouse, Elmsfield Business Centre, Worcester Road, Chipping Norton, Oxfordshire OX7 5XL**

Transport and Communications

Waste and Recycling

Nothing gets wasted in the natural world – things just cycle round and round. But cheap energy and a misguided use of technology have led us to manufacture numerous "long-lasting" products that are outside natural cycles and will not break down for millions of years. The result has been a quest for ever larger holes in the ground in which to dispose of unwanted items that no longer meet our needs but, of course, remain as long lasting as the day when we bought them! There is massive scope for reusing what we have more efficiently before we even think about reducing our real standard of living. If you don't want something anymore then pass it on – it's about not having to make a new thing when one already exists ... cycling objects around society using libraries; car boot sales; charity shops; auctions; jumble sales; Freegle; and eBay. Once you step out of the mindset that says "Only new will do" then it's easy and opens up all sorts of creative avenues for reusing leftovers and blending them together. Basic repair skills will be the most sought after in the future. The comprehensive recycling infrastructure that now exists is a real step forward but is not, in itself, very sustainable because it needs large amounts of energy to move the materials around and then reprocess them. Metal recycling will probably always be viable but many things that are now recycled will no longer be as ubiquitous if lack of cheap oil means that the mass-production society that generates them is no longer able to churn out the same volumes. For instance, we might do well to push for a system of standardised glass containers that could be collected and reused very locally rather than shipping used glass around, then melting it down to make a constant supply of new items.

RECYCLING, RUBBISH AND WASTE

Household waste and refuse collection services are now controlled by Cornwall Council. The former district councils had contracts with waste management companies or provided services themselves.

Cornwall Council has now awarded a new waste collection contract to Cory Environmental. A kerbside recycling collection service is offered to every household and this can be used to recycle over 40% of waste.

Web: **http://www.cornwall.gov.uk**
Email: **refuseandrecycling@cornwall.gov.uk**
Phone: **03001 234 141**

CORNWALL SCRAP STORE

Cornwall Scrap Store is a fantastic resource, stocking an amazing range of interesting, unusual and unique materials and products, which can be

used in art, craft and play activities for all ages. They collect this valuable 'scrap' from businesses around the county and rescue it from being dumped in local landfill sites, making it available to their members - absolutely free! Open to schools, nurseries, play-schemes, community groups, pensioners groups, carnival committees, youth groups, scouts, church groups, village halls, parent and toddler groups, sports clubs, charities, students, families and even individuals. They also have wallpaper, paint, tiles, carpet, fabrics and much more. There's a low annual membership fee. Also in St Austell.

Web: **http://www.cornwallscrapstore.co.uk**
Phone: **01726 821 161**
Address: **Church Road, Pool, Redruth, Cornwall TR15 3PT**

CORNWALL WASTE ACTION

Cornwall Waste Action is involved in a range of project activity. Projects and partnerships include  composting, beachcleans, local food growing, capacity building and the Community Waste Art Project. It also provides consultancy services for the public and private sector as well as third sector organisations and civil society groups. These include compost doctors, waste audits, project management and feasibility studies.

Web: http://www.cornwallwasteaction.org.uk
Email: info@wasteaction.org.uk

FREE FOR ALL

The West Cornwall Green Party have instigated very popular 'Free for All' events, where people can share unwanted goods and help themselves  to those that other people bring along. Free for Alls now happen at the Guildhall, St Ives on the first Saturday in March and October.

Email: tim@timandrewes.com
Phone: 01736 795 387

GOFA - GOOD OLD FURNITURE AVAILABLE

GOFA is a furniture and electrical appliance reuse project based in Penzance. They provide donated furniture and household electrical goods at affordable prices to  people on low incomes so that they can furnish their homes. Donating to or buying from GOFA helps everyone.

Web: http://www.gofa.org.uk
Email: keith@gofa.org.uk
Phone: 01736 369 847
Address: Ellis Square, Voundervour Lane, Penzance TR18 4UH

Waste and Recycling

HAYLE AND ST IVES FREEGLE

The Hayle & St Ives group started in June 2006 and moved to Freegle in September 2009. The group borders Penzance Freegle, and is open to all who want to "recycle" that special something rather than throw it away. Local non-profit groups are welcome to participate!

Web: http://uk.groups.yahoo.com/group/HayleFreegle/
Email: HayleFreegle-owner@yahoogroups.co.uk

LOCAL CAR BOOT SALES

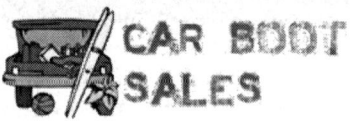

Car boot sales are another way that pre-enjoyed goods can get a whole new life! Here are all the local ones that we know about - we've not published times as it's always a complicated business. Contact the organisers directly for more information.

Gulval
- Gulval Cricket Club, St Ives Road, Gulval, Penzance
  June to October, Fridays

Hayle
- Hayle Rugby Club Rugby Football Club, Memorial Park,
  Marsh Lane, Hayle TR27 4PS. All year, Sundays (01736 757157)

Ludgvan
- Ludgvan Sports and Social Club, Ludgvan, Penzance TR20 8ES
  All year, Mondays (07974 562959)

Penzance
- Penzance and Newlyn Rugby Football Club, Alexandra Road,
  Penzance TR18 4LY. April to October, Thursdays (01736 364044)

Rosudgeon
- Rosudgeon Sports and Social Club, Rosudgeon TR20 9QE
  April to October, Wednesdays (01736 763773)
  May to September, Fridays (01736 763773)

St Ives
- Guildhall, Street-an-Pol, St Ives
  All year, Wednesdays (01736 757625)

LOCAL CHARITY SHOPS

Charity shops are one of the best ways that our society has to recycle goods ... and somebody else benefits along the way! Here are  all the local charity shops that we know about - let us know if we've missed any.

Hayle
- Cornwall Animal Hospital Charity Shop, 23 Beatrice Terrace, Hayle TR27 4ED. http://www.cancerresearchuk.org

Penzance
- Barnardo's, 10/13 Causewayhead, Penzance TR18 2SN 01736 365148 - http://www.barnardos.org.uk
- British Heart Foundation, 90 Market Jew Street, Penzance 01736 363403 - http://www.bhf.org.uk
- Cancer Research UK, 74 Causewayhead, Penzance 01736 351549 - http://www.cancerresearchuk.org
- Cornwall Animal Hospital Charity Shop, The Terrace, 40 Market Jew Street, Penzance TR18 2HX 01736 351549 - http://www.cornwallanimalhospital.org
- Our Stuff Our Shop Community, The Lescudjack Centre, Penmere Close, Penzance TR18 3PE 01736 334857
- Oxfam, 15c Causewayhead, Penzance TR18 2SN 01736 367666 - http://www.oxfam.org.uk
- Scope, 22-23 Causewayhead, Penzance TR18 2SP 01736 364142 - http://www.scope.org.uk
- Sue Ryder, Unit 1, 114-117 Market Jew Street, Penzance TR18 2LD. http://www.suerydercare.org

St Ives
- Cornwall Hospice Care, 1 Tregenna Hill, St Ives TR26 1SE 01736 798667 - http://www.cornish-hospices.co.uk
- Save The Children, 6 High Street, St Ives TR26 1RR 01736 793619 - http://www.savethechildren.org.uk
- Sue Ryder Care, 15 Tregenna Place, Saint Ives TR26 1SD 01736 793526 - http://www.suerydercare.org

St Just
- Age UK, Meneghy, 27 Fore Street, St Just, Penzance TR19 7LJ 01736 788265 - http://www.ageuk.org.uk

Waste and Recycling

LOCAL LIBRARIES

Libraries are one of the most sophisticated forms of organised recycling that we have. Use them or lose them.

Web: http://www.cornwall.gov.uk

Hayle

• Hayle Library, Commercial Road, Hayle TR27 4DE
  hayle.library@cornwall.gov.uk
• Hayle Toy Library, Hayle Children's Centre, Bodriggy Street, Hayle TR27 4ND. 01736 759058

Penzance

• Morrab Road, Penzance TR18 4EY
  penzance.library@cornwall.gov.uk
• Penzance Toy Library, Penzance Children's Centre, Penmere Close, Penzance TR18 3PE. 01736 334850

St Ives

• St Ives Library, Gabriel Street, St Ives TR26 2LX
  stives.library@cornwall.gov.uk
• St Ives Toy Library, St Ives Children's Centre, Trenwith Burrows, St Ives TR26 1DJ. 01736 798509

St Just

• St Just Library, Market Street, St Just TR19 7HX
  stjust.library@cornwall.gov.uk

PENWITH WOODLAND BURIAL PLACE

Rose Farm is a peaceful setting in which to be buried. A tree is planted on every grave and this, in turn, helps the environment and provides habitat for wild life. The Pets' Memorial Gardens which also exists at Rose Farm was established

in 1988. Human burials have taken place there since 2000.

Web: http://www.woodlandburialplace.co.uk

Email: info@woodlandburialplace.co.uk

Phone: 01736 731 310

Address: Rose Farm, Chyenhal, Drift, Penzance TR19 6AN

PENZANCE FREEGLE

Penzance Freegle covers Lands End to Penzance and surrounding area up to the borders of the Hayle & St Ives Group. Open to all who want to "recycle" rather than throw it  away. Local non-profit groups also welcome to participate. Everything posted must be free and keeping something out of landfill.

Web: http://groups.yahoo.com/group/PenzanceFreegle/

Email: PenzanceFreegle-owner@yahoogroups.com

RECYCLE NOW

Find out what items you can recycle and where recycling banks are located in the local area.

Your local recycling banks

Web: http://www.recyclenow.com

Badgers Cross
- Eddie Woods, Badgers Cross Workshop, Badgers Cross, Penzance TR20 8XE
  Car Oil

Halsetown
- The Halsetown Inn, Halsetown, St Ives TR26 3NA
  Glass Bottles/Jars

Hayle
- Commercial Road Car Park, Hayle TR27 4DE
  Glass Bottles/Jars, Metal Food and Drink Cans, Mixed Paper, All Textiles, All Plastic Bottles, Books
- Foundry Square Car Park, Hayle TR27 4HH
  Metal Food and Drink Cans

Long Rock
- Morrisons Car Park, Long Rock Business Park, Long Rock, Penzance TR18 3RF
  Glass Bottles/Jars, Metal Food and Drink Cans, Books, Cardboard, Mixed Paper, All Plastic Bottles, All Textiles

Marazion
- Kings Road Car Park, Marazion, Penzance TR17 0EJ
  Glass Bottles/Jars

Waste and Recycling

Pendeen
- Boscaswell Car Park, Pendeen, Penzance TR19 7EP
Mixed Paper, Glass Bottles/Jars, Metal Food and Drink Cans

Penzance
- Penzance Harbour TR18 4BD
Glass Bottles/Jars, Metal Food and Drink Cans, Mixed Paper
- St Erbyns Car Park, Clarence Street, Penzance TR18 2NU
Glass Bottles/Jars, Metal Food and Drink Cans, Mixed Paper,
All Textiles
- Tesco Car Park, Eastern Green, Penzance TR18 3DU
Glass Bottles/Jars, Metal Food and Drink Cans, Mixed Paper,
All Textiles, All Plastic Bottles, Books, Cardboard, Plastic Carrier Bags
- Tesco, 104 Market Jew St, Penzance TR18 2LE
Domestic Batteries
- Wherrytown Car Park, Promenade, Penzance TR18 4NP
Glass Bottles/Jars, Metal Food and Drink Cans, Mixed Paper,
All Textiles

Porthcurno
- Porthurno Car Park TR19 6JY
Glass Bottles/Jars, Metal Food and Drink Cans

Rosudgeon
- Prussia Cove Road TR20 9QE
Glass Bottles/Jars, Metal Food and Drink Cans, Mixed Paper,
All Plastic Bottles, Books, Cardboard

Sennen
- Sennen Car Park TR19 7AD
Metal Food and Drink Cans

St Buryan
- St Buryan Community Centre, St Buryan, Penzance TR19 6BT
Glass Bottles/Jars, Metal Food and Drink Cans, Mixed Paper,
All Plastic Bottles, Cardboard

St Erth
- HAYLE HOUSEHOLD WASTE AND RECYCLING CENTRE,
ST ERTH, HAYLE, CORNWALL TR27 6LA
Asbestos, Cans, Car and household batteries, Cardboard,
Clothes and textiles, Cooking oil, Energy saving lightbulbs,
Engine oil, Fridges and freezers, Fluorescent tubes, Gas bottles,
Glass, Green/Garden waste, Household chemicals under
5 litres, Household waste, Items for resale, Metal, Newspaper
and magazines, Plastic bottles, Rubble, Small electrical items,
Televisions and Monitors, Tyres, Wood

- Star Inn, St Erth, Hayle TR27 6HP
  Glass Bottles/Jars

St Erth Praze
- Smugglers Inn, 3 Clais Road, St Erth Praze, Hayle TR27 6EG
  Glass Bottles/Jars, Metal Food and Drink Cans

St Ives
- Tesco Car Park, St Ives Road, Carbis Bay, St Ives TR26 2PN
  Domestic Batteries, Glass Bottles/Jars, Metal Food and Drink Cans,
  Mixed Paper, All Textiles, All Plastic Bottles, Cardboard, Plastic
  Carrier Bags
- Travis Perkins, Unit 2b, Penbeagle Ind Est, St Ives TR26 2JH
  Domestic Batteries
- Trenwith Car Park, St Ives TR26 2PN
  Glass Bottles/Jars, Metal Food and Drink Cans, Mixed Paper,
  All Textiles, All Plastic Bottles, Cardboard

St Just
- Lafrowda Car Park, St Just, Penzance TR19 7RY
  Glass Bottles/Jars, Metal Food and Drink Cans, Mixed Paper, All Textiles,
  All Plastic Bottles, Cardboard
- St Just Rugby Football Club, New Road,
  Tregeseal, St Just TR19 7PF
  Glass Bottles/Jars

**Waste and
Recycling**

SURFERS AGAINST SEWAGE

SAS protects the health of recreational water users from sewage polluted water. Scientific studies have consistently highlighted that those using

beaches, lakes or rivers for sports are most at risk of falling sick from an illness associated with sewage polluted water. They are also seeking improvements to the combined sewer overflow (CSOs) systems that pollute recreational waters all too frequently, usually after heavy rainfall. Much of current investment has ignored or disregarded the impacts of climate change, in particular changing weather patterns that will result in increased flows of water into and out of the sewage works without treatment because there is not enough capacity to store the sewage.

Web: http://www.sas.org.uk

Phone: 01872 553 001

Address: Unit 2, Wheal Kitty Workshops, St Agnes TR5 0RD

THE GREEN WASTE COMPANY

The Green Waste Company is a local, family-run business with expertise in waste management. They provide customers with a wide range of options to meet their waste and recycling needs. They recycle large quantities of green and wood waste annually under their 25,000 tonne waste management licence, and and were among the first of the waste-handling companies in the UK to achieve Compost Association Accreditation. They accept: green waste from commercial contractors; waste wood; demolition timber; pallets; and wood offcuts; and various plastics and farm plastics. They bulk sell: woodchips for outdoor events, mulch for landscaping schemes; and sawdust bedding for agricultural animals. Also bulk compost for gardens, sports fields and agriculture.

Web: http://www.greenwastecompany.com

Email: info@greenwastecompany.com

Phone: 01736 752 393

Address: Splattenridden, Hayle, Cornwall TR27 6LH

Waste and Recycling

Postscript

We hope that this book will be useful to you and that awareness of the huge number of positive things that are happening in the Penwith area will inspire you. It's our first attempt so please forgive any errors or omissions and don't take it personally if your favourite project has been missed out. If you know of other new or existing organisations that might be listed in future then please inform us at the earliest opportunity – they can be added to the online directory straight away then be included in the next printed edition whenever that is published.

One of our greatest regrets is that this book is not being printed locally. After all rebuilding the local economy is what Transition Penwith is meant to be all about, isn't it? The reason is that this publication is produced using quite sophisticated technology available from only a tiny number of suppliers in the UK. The, so-called, print-on-demand process means that incredibly small runs can be manufactured to order. The major benefits of this are that there is hardly any financial risk; very low capital requirement; and – most importantly – no possibility of being left with boxes and boxes of unsold books which then have to go into landfill when they are out of date!

We think that the price is worth paying and hope that it will enable us to produce future editions that have more of the feel of a yearbook – flagging up definite events, featuring articles and publishing research results as well as news items about recent positive developments in Penwith's transition to a sustainable future. Perhaps something you have started as a result of being inspired by *Resilient Penwith* will be featured in a future edition!

About Transition Penwith

Transition Penwith was created in 2006 when local councillor Jennifer Grey invited American journalist, educator and expert on oil depletion Richard Heinberg to give a public address at Penzance Town Hall. 350 people turned up – a broad spectrum of West Cornwall's diverse community including all the town mayors in their full regalia! Penwith is the district at the far south-western tip of Britain including the towns of Hayle, Penzance, St Ives and St Just as well as the numerous villages and hamlets of the Lands End Peninsula and the western part of Mounts Bay. It loosely covers the operating area of the former Penwith District Council and is really a "Transition District" rather than a Transition Town. Consequently it acts more as a support organisation for localised transition projects, hoping to nurture and fertilise as well as aiming to reproduce the successes of one locality in other areas across the district. If you've come across this book as a visitor to Penwith and would like to know about transition initiatives in your own part of the world then take a look at this website:

www.transitionnetwork.org

Disclaimer

The information contained in this book is for general information purposes only. While Transition Penwith has endeavoured to obtain information that is up to date and correct, we make no representations or warranties of any kind, express or implied, about the completeness, accuracy, reliability, suitability or availability with respect to the information, products or services contained in the book. Any reliance you place on such information is therefore strictly at your own risk.

Acknowledgements and gratitude

Resilient Penwith is a project that has come from the Core Group of Transition Penwith. The main contributors have been Jonathan How; Lesley Bradley-Peer; and Chris Abbott with other contributions coming from: Kelsey Michael; David Smart Knight; Rob Pickering; Joanne Schofield; Llyn Aubrey; Marilyn Gibson; Colin Curbishley; Juliet Wallis; and Tim Andrewes.

Transition Penwith wishes to thank the Sustainable Energy Communities project run by Community Energy Plus and funded by West Cornwall Local Action Group for support with producing this book.

Lightning Source UK Ltd.
Milton Keynes UK
UKOW040949160612

194539UK00005B/3/P